THE HOLOCAUST MUSEUM IN WASHINGTON

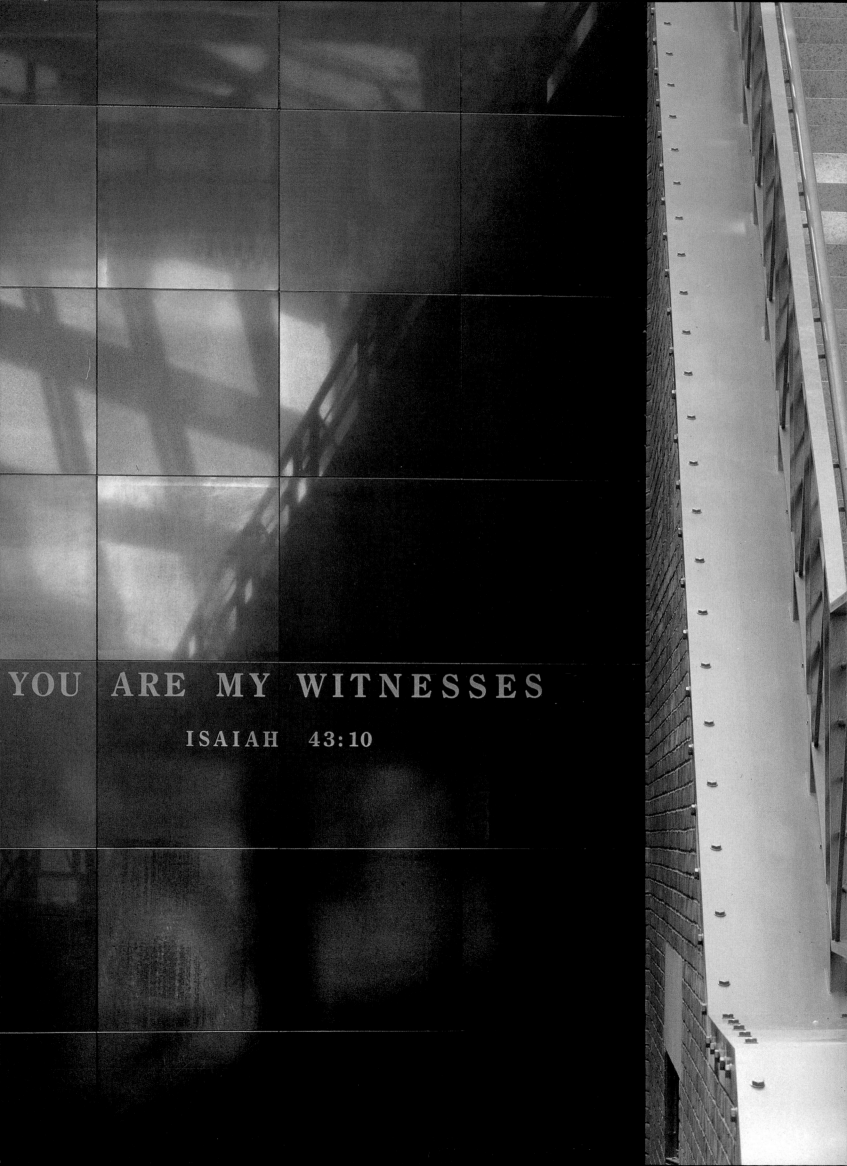

YOU ARE MY WITNESSES

ISAIAH 43:10

THE HOLOCAUST MUSEUM IN WASHINGTON

JESHAJAHU WEINBERG AND RINA ELIELI

IN COLLABORATION WITH

THE UNITED STATES HOLOCAUST MEMORIAL MUSEUM

This book is dedicated to all those
who contributed to the creation of the
United States Holocaust Memorial Museum.

First published in the United States of America in 1995 by
RIZZOLI INTERNATIONAL PUBLICATIONS, INC.
300 Park Avenue South
New York, New York 10010

Library of Congress Cataloging-in-Publication Data

Weinberg, Jeshajahu.
    The Holocaust Museum in Washington / by Jeshajahu Weinberg and
Rina Elieli.
        p. cm.
    Includes index.
    ISBN 0-8478-1906-X — ISBN 0-8478-1907-8 (pbk.)
    1. U.S. Holocaust Memorial Museum. 2. Holocaust, Jewish (1939-
1945)—Museums—Washington (D.C.) I. Elieli, Rina. II. Title.
D804.3.W3947 1995
940.53' 18' 074753—dc20   95-1622
                                                            CIP

Designed by Alex Castro

Printed in Japan

Page 1: Skylight in the Hall of Remembrance.

Pages 2 and 3: The Museum is situated between the Bureau
of Engraving and Printing to the south and the red-brick
Auditor's Building to the north. The semidetached, six-sided
Hall of Remembrance stands as the nation's memorial to the
victims of the Holocaust.

Page 4: The marble wall in the Hall of Witness.

Page 6: Eisenhower Plaza and entrance to the Museum.

TABLE OF CONTENTS

HOW FAR WE HAVE TRAVELED during the span of only a single lifetime in our understanding of what a museum can be!

When I was young and casting about for ways to deal with the dark atmosphere of the then raging Second World War and the stupefying news of the annihilation of European Jewry that had begun to drift into our New York apartment, I discovered, among other marvelous things, the exquisite world of museums.

The Metropolitan Museum of Art, the Museum of Modern Art, the Brooklyn Museum, and other such settings large and small, seemed to me wondrous modernist versions of Greek and Roman temples for the display of ageless beauty—those surroundings became for me a kind of second home, places in which to calm the troubled heart.

During the years that followed, the sense of a museum as a sacred repository for the artifacts of human creativity was reinforced each time I made my way through the galleries and corridors of the British Museum, the Louvre, the Jeu de Paume—through all the hushed echoing rooms in which were displayed millennia of the treasures of humankind. I craved such places. And for years I simply assumed that was what a museum was: a locus of beauty. Until the day I visited the Museum of the Diaspora in Israel, viewed with wonder its displays, and met Jeshajahu Weinberg, the man who had thought it into life.

I saw a short, soft-spoken, seemingly unassuming person, and it was rather difficult at first for me to imagine so vast and audacious a concept originating with so unpretentious an individual. All the throb and rhythm of a people's troubled history exhibited vividly and truthfully in a way that enabled the visitor to interact, ask questions, talk to the displays, enter deeply into the exhibition, take on the identities of various personalities, make fateful choices as to one's own destiny—what an audacious idea for a museum! How alive it all was! One went away feeling not the soaring serenity that is the aftermath of a visit, say, to the Musée d'Orsay, but the rooted sense of having deeply experienced the world. To be sure, one was tired, but it was the healthy fatigue of profound involvement with truth, of hours spent in a transfiguring encounter with one's deepest sense of self.

Years later, a chance encounter with someone from the upper echelons of the *Washington Post* brought me into contact with yet another Jeshajahu Weinberg concept for a museum: the United States Holocaust Memorial Museum in Washington.

When I saw that museum for the first time, it sat on tables in an office, roof and outer walls missing, inner walls exposed. It was a maquette, a miniature, a scale model of the projected interior that gave barely a hint of its future as an extraordinary architectural creation, let alone how it would finally impart the charged history of horror that was its essential reason for being. The building itself, in an early stage of construction, stood on a nearby street, its raw girders like an intricate steel webbing, workers scrambling about its entrails, the noise of construction at times quite deafening as I navigated through wires, cables, tools and dust. It was impossible for me to envisage the final shape the place would have, its future face to the world.

I remember asking one of the workers at the building site what he thought about the future museum.

"There oughta be one in every town in the country," he replied. "Maybe keep us from killing people this way again."

Prisoner uniforms displayed in the Museum's Permanent Exhibition.

The next time I visited the museum was about a month before it opened its doors to the public. Then I saw clearly its awesome monumentality: the play of forms from the world of death transformed so brilliantly by its team of architects into an art booth disturbingly raw and profoundly moving; the weave of its corridors and exhibits; the tranquillity of spaces given over to respite and meditation.

The third time I saw the museum was on the day of the pre-opening ceremony that took place at Arlington National Cemetery. The entrance march of the survivors, the speeches, the readings, the Danes who talked in the most unheroic terms of the part they played in the rescue of Jews, as if wondering what the fuss was all about, the flapping of the flags in a suddenly rising wind, the menacing skies . . . and the rows and rows of American graves. . . .

One is stunned by the sheer enormity of the enterprise. Consider the tangled issues: its mission, its cost, its site, its contents, its commitment to truth. Consider the thousands of individuals and institutions caught up in its creation: lay people, many of them Holocaust survivors; professional staff; political figures; American government officials; the vast public; the fund-raising and public-relations personnel; the architects; the foreign governments. Years of thought, years of effort, years of day and night involvement.

And now—the dust of beginning has settled. The opening ceremonies are at an end, the speeches have concluded, the participants have returned to their homes, many among the original staff have gone on to other tasks. The museum has passed into a living presence and is one of the most visited federal museums in our country.

The first act in the drama—the creation of the museum—is over. Having come to an end, that act now deserves very careful documentation, a history, a recording of its events for future perusal and consideration.

This book is that record.

Among the most estimable qualities of this volume is its forthrightness, the candor with which it presents all sides in the high drama: the debates, the early errors, the stops and starts, the domestic and international lobbying—the many intricate moves and maneuverings that went into the making of this museum.

Also considered in this book is the fact that the second act is taking place during the museum's current life: the time of changeover from the dust of construction to the grit of actuality, from fluid often informal teamwork to dignified bureaucratic institution.

In this second act the public now plays a major part—as spectator, as participant, as sounding board, as the potential originator of new ideas, and as transmitter of the museum's narrative to those who have not yet visited its exhibitions.

It takes an immense measure of courage to enter a museum which is not about beauty but about grim and profound truths concerning the more appalling aspects of humankind. That so many millions of people are prepared to encounter this very different kind of museum is a clear testament of hope for our species.

What a singular experience the United States Holocaust Memorial Museum has become—for us today and, one hopes, for all the future generations of this republic!

CHAIM POTOK
March 1995

Facing Page: Section of the model of the Auschwitz crematoria made by the sculptor Mieczyslaw Stobierski for the Museum.

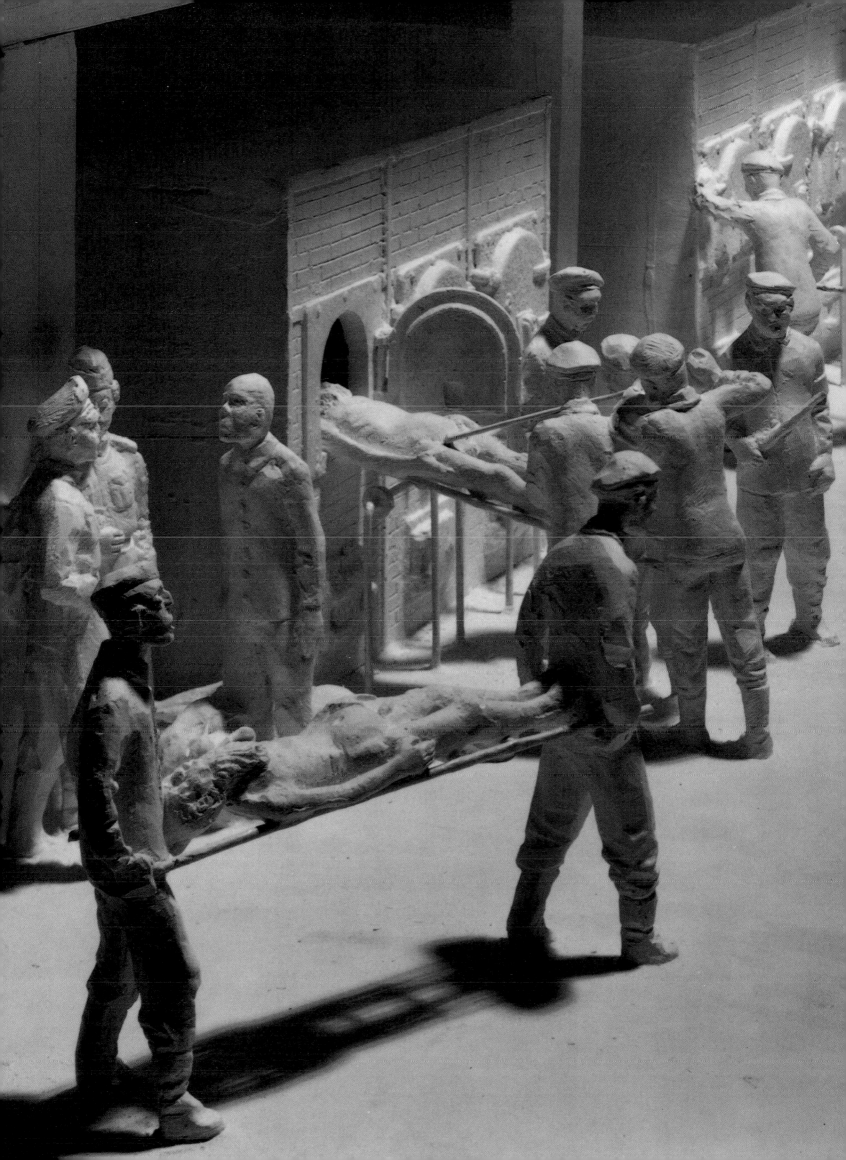

PREFACE

THIS BOOK TELLS THE STORY of the United States Holocaust Memorial Museum in Washington, D.C. It describes the nature of the Museum, and explains the process that led to its creation. It tries in its text and its illustrations to present a comprehensive picture of the Museum's unusual character. It is an analysis and an inside story. One of the many aspects of the Museum's special character is that it cannot be adequately served by an annotated catalogue. It can only be described.

This book is intended for many audiences. It is written for those who visit the Museum, as a souvenir; for those who will visit it, as an introduction; and for those who have not visited it, as an invitation. It is written for all those who, one way or another, contributed to the creation of the Museum. It is also written for museum professionals who want to get acquainted with the methods and design strategies that allowed this unusual museum to grow from abstract dream to three-dimensional reality.

The book was written by Jeshajahu Weinberg, who was the founding director of the Museum, responsible for its planning phase and the first stages of its operation, in collaboration with Rina Elieli, a consultant to the Director who participated in the development of the Museum in the critical time prior to its opening to the public. Why was the book written jointly? Frequently it is difficult to describe one's own work, and a more objective partner for whom nothing is self-understood can make possible the composition of a complete story. Rina fulfilled this important function of creative provocation.

Although the book has been written and published at the request of the Museum, the opinions expressed should not be understood as representing the official point of view of the Museum. They only represent the point of view of the authors.

The Museum was the creation of a wonderful team of highly talented and devoted people—staff members, council members, consultants, and contractors—who, together with an ingenious architect, made it happen. To all of them the Director expresses gratitude for their creative cooperation.

Only a few names can be found in the book. It was impossible to mention the many hundreds who made meaningful contributions, but it should never be forgotten that it was not one person, nor only a handful of people who deserve credit for the creation of the Museum.

We are deeply grateful to all those who accompanied and assisted us in our effort to bring this book to completion: to Arnold Kramer, the photographic editor, and Alex Castro, the book's designer, who applied their creative talents to the visual aspects of the book, and to Beth Redlich who assisted them in this endeavor; to Kathryn Hill, who authored the captions for all illustrations; to Maureen Graney, whose editorial contribution was invaluable; to our good friends Sara Bloomfield, Elaine Heumann Gurian, Jeffrey LaRiche, Dalia Frieberger, and Claude Faucheux, who read the manuscript and made many intelligent and extremely important corrective comments; to Yehiam Halevy and William Parsons, who suggested meaningful corrections relating to the activities of their respective departments, the Wexner Learning Center and the Education Department; to Ron Goldfarb, who made important comments and whose good offices were crucial in the critical stages of bringing this book to fruition; to Betsy Chock, who diligently helped us with research and with much admirable patience gave us efficient administrative assistance in the preparation of the manuscript; and last but not least to Judith Joseph, President and CEO of Rizzoli International Publications, without whose continuous encouragement and understanding this book could not have been written and published.

Shoes from victims of the Majdanek Concentration Camp near Lublin, Poland.

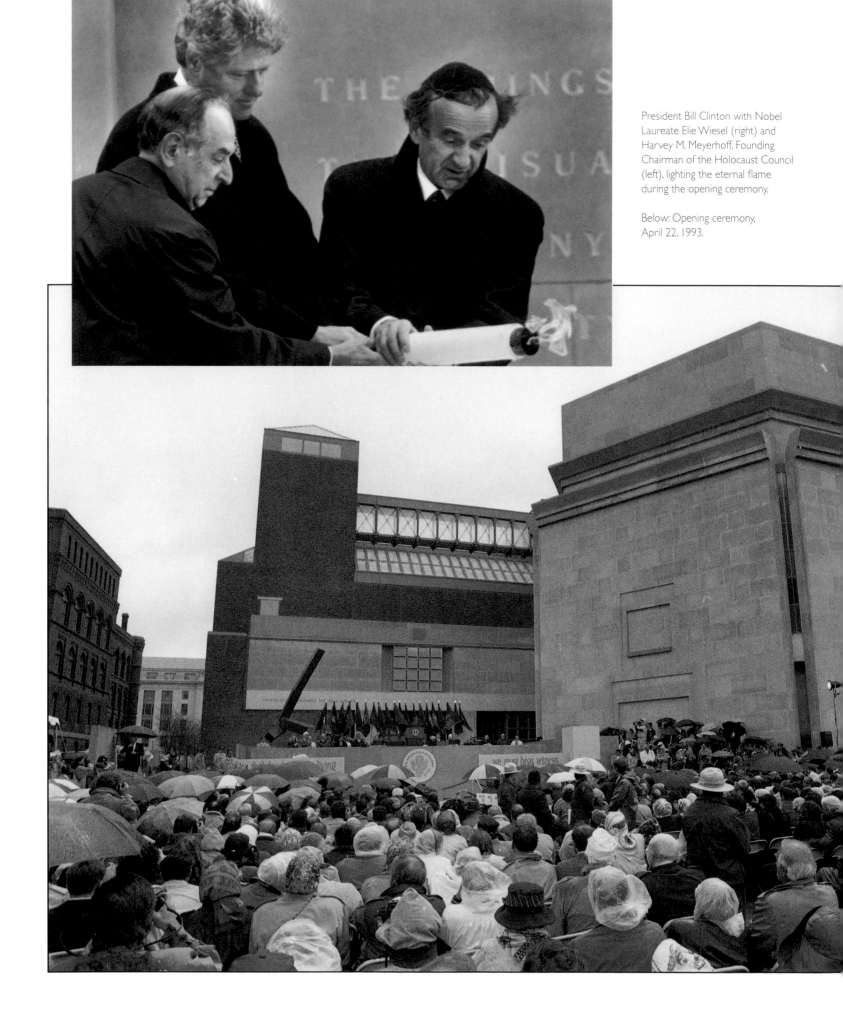

President Bill Clinton with Nobel Laureate Elie Wiesel (right) and Harvey M. Meyerhoff, Founding Chairman of the Holocaust Council (left), lighting the eternal flame during the opening ceremony.

Below: Opening ceremony, April 22, 1993.

CREATING A LIVING MUSEUM

The United States Holocaust Memorial Museum was opened by President Bill Clinton on April 22, 1993. It was in the middle of spring, but on this particular day, the weather adapted itself to the spirit of the occasion. It was freezing cold. The thousands of people who came to attend the opening found themselves caught in stormy wind and rain. They had come from throughout the United States as well as from overseas. Among the participants were heads of state both from countries that were involved in the Holocaust and from some that were not.

A great number of Holocaust survivors were among those who attended the opening ceremony. These very special guests had been involved in the creation of the Museum: they had donated their memorabilia from the days of the Holocaust, documented their personal experiences in testimonies, contributed funds, and urged others who were not at all involved in the Holocaust to contribute. The survivors had provided the building blocks for the creation of what they regarded as the realization of their deepest need: to let the world know.

With the opening of the United States Holocaust Memorial Museum, the survivors saw their dream come true. Their story was now told to the world by the American people, in a governmental museum established in the United States's capital as an important addition to the community of American museums. The survivors regarded it as their museum. They were not the only ones whose support was crucial for the creation of the Museum, but were it not for them, it would never have been created.

The Holocaust Museum is a history museum, though not a history museum in the traditional sense. It takes as its point of departure a historical narrative. It is perhaps most accurately called a narrative museum, because its display is organized along a story line.

The story told in the Museum describes the roles of the actors who were involved in the Holocaust: the perpetrators, the victims, the bystanders, the rescuers, and the liberators. The victims wanted the world to know. The perpetrators wanted the world not to know. The bystanders wanted the world not to know that they knew.

In the ghettos, in the death camps, on their way to the gas chambers, the victims were isolated from the entire world. It was their last wish that the world know what they went through. When the historian Emanuel Ringelblum recorded the happenings in the Warsaw ghetto day by day, he did so for posterity. On the eve of the final annihilation of the ghetto, he buried all records and documents in metal containers and milk cans so they would be found after the war, after his death and the death of all other members of his historical society. So they would let the world know.

Survivors often say that those who were not there will never understand. Not even the most imaginative description of the Holocaust can truly reflect the horror of those days. No description can reenact the emotions of victims and survivors. And still, even survivors who emphasize the inability of any narrative to fully portray their sufferings, even they wanted the story to be told, in spite of all the inevitable shortcomings in the narrative reflection of historical truth.

After liberation, those who did not perish, the survivors, felt compelled to tell their story even though they knew the story could not be fully told. Moreover, in their post-Holocaust life, they realized that it was difficult to find an open ear for what they wanted to tell. It was a new era. A new life was beginning in the world, and nobody wanted the horrors of the past to interfere. Thus the first postwar decades were characterized by what one can call a "conspiracy of silence" by perpetrators, victims, and bystanders alike.

Memorials were erected by survivors and those who were close to them, but memorials do not tell the story, they only serve as reminders for those who already know. There were site museums and monuments, established at the very places where the horrible events took place, but those, too, hardly gave a comprehensive picture of the historic event. Israel, the Jewish state, which considers itself custodian of Jewish memory, had created Yad Vashem, the Holocaust Martyrs' and Heroes' Memorial, and also the Ghetto Fighters House and several small Holocaust museums. These were primarily expressions of the Jewish urge to remember Jewish pain and suffering—never to forget.

Visitors queueing to enter the Museum.

Now, with the opening of the United States Holocaust Memorial Museum, the story was presented and validated with the authoritative voice of a federal museum by the American people. This presentation was both the realization of the survivors' dream and an admission of the bystanders' historic guilt. America, as a nation, represents simultaneously the bystanders, who were guilty for not having done what could have been to save victims, and the bystanders, who fulfilled the moral command, to stand up against Hitler.

The Museum reflects not only the historic event of the Holocaust, involving victims and perpetrators, but also the story of the bystanders, the rescuers, and liberators. In this way it constitutes an act of public self-criticism of the American nation. Only in a democracy like America could a governmental museum include in its presentation, beside the well deserved recognition and praise, such harsh self-criticism.

The unusual nature of the Museum's opening event revealed that it is more than a memorial, much more than a museum. It is also an institution operating at a high level of public, political sensitivity and moral responsibility. Because of this, it became a place of pilgrimage soon after it opened its doors to the public. Thousands of people who, walking in silence together through the exhibition galleries, are confronted with the images of extreme human tragedy, undergo an experience similar to that of pilgrims walking together to a sacred place.

Both on the level of museum methodology and from the aspect of a museum's function in society, the United States Holocaust Memorial Museum is a museum of a different kind.

THE EDUCATIONAL MISSION

The Museum believes that one of the Holocaust's fundamental lessons is that to be a bystander is to share in the guilt. This lesson is applicable to the contemporary problems of society and to the behavior of individuals. Within any society, groups and individuals are constantly confronted with the destructive potential human beings possess. Only the intervention of the bystander can help society to become more human.

The most crucial aspect of the Museum's educational role is demonstrating the applicability of the moral lessons learned from the Holocaust to current and future events. This is indeed what the Museum is all about: creating an encounter between the visitor and this moral imperative. What makes this educational endeavor a complex and difficult task is that it takes place within a pluralistic, multiethnic society accustomed to seeing the Holocaust as an ethnic event that took place on foreign soil and concerned primarily the Jews of Europe. To make this event meaningful for the totality of American society and for the world, the Museum has to reveal the Holocaust's universal significance beyond any limited ethnic experience. Teaching the lessons of the Holocaust implies, therefore, abstract conceptualization and "universalization" of the moral conclusions stemming from a concrete, unique, seemingly ethnic event. Because of its almost inconceivably strong impact, the Holocaust has the character of a brutal, overwhelming metaphor for all historic events of genocidal character, while always remaining the concrete historic event.

In the process of becoming exposed to the Museum's exhibits and activities, visitors thus find themselves positioned between two poles: between the concrete and the abstract, the historical and the metaphoric, the unique and the universal. The tension and discourse between these poles is inherent in the essence of the Museum and its educational work. One can say that, at any single moment, the educational process is taking place in the space between one pole and the other. To preserve the overwhelming power of the concrete event and, at the same time, the symbolic, universal implications inherent in it, there should never be an attempt at resolving the tension between the poles.

The Museum's educational responsibility is to help visitors apply the metaphoric meaning embedded in Holocaust history to their contemporary experience as individuals and as members of society. To best achieve this, thematic neatness has to be observed in the depiction of the historic event as presented in the exhibition. The exhibition has to be limited to the historic event, so as not to obscure its metaphoric universality.

The Museum's attitude to relevant contemporary events is linked to this approach. The Museum must remain a museum of the Holocaust; it should not become a museum of genocide, nor a museum of human rights. A very delicate demarcation line separates the appropriate use of the metaphor from its abuse.

Inside the Permanent Exhibition.

The very term "Holocaust" is being increasingly misused as a description for a variety of events, thus diluting the overwhelming uniqueness of the Holocaust of the Second World War: the bureaucratically organized murder of six million Jews and millions of other victims to whose memory the Museum is devoted.

HOW IT ALL BEGAN

On September 27, 1979, the President's Commission on the Holocaust, chaired by Elie Wiesel, submitted to President Jimmy Carter a recommendation to establish "a living memorial" composed of three principal components: a National Holocaust Memorial/Museum; an educational foundation, and a Committee on Conscience.

At the White House in 1978: President Jimmy Carter, holding a copy of the report of the President's Commission on the Holocaust, with Benjamin Meed, President of the American Gathering, and his wife, Vladka Meed.

Facing page: Bridges over the Hall of Witness.

The Commission had been appointed by the President on November 1, 1978; it counted among its thirty-four members leaders of the survivor community, eminent Holocaust historians, Senators, and Congressmen as well as other public figures. It was charged with the task of submitting a report "with respect to the establishment and maintenance of an appropriate memorial to those who perished in the Holocaust . . . and to recommend appropriate ways for the nation to commemorate April 28 and 29, 1979, which the Congress has resolved shall be 'Days of Remembrance of Victims of the Holocaust'."

On October 7, 1980, Congress decided unanimously to establish "as an independent Federal establishment the United States Holocaust Memorial Council." The Council was charged with three tasks:

1. To "provide for appropriate ways for the Nation to commemorate the Days of Remembrance, as an annual, national, civic commemoration of the Holocaust, and . . . encourage and sponsor appropriate observance of such Days of Remembrance throughout the United States."
2. To "plan, construct, and observe the operation of a permanent living memorial museum to the Holocaust, in cooperation with the Secretary of the Interior and other Federal agencies. . . ."
3. To "develop a plan for carrying out the recommendations of the President's Commission on the Holocaust in its report to the President of September 27, 1979. . . ."

The Council, which remains the Museum's governing body, consists of sixty-eight members: fifty-five appointees of the President of the United States; five members of the Senate; five members of the U.S. House of Representatives, and three ex officio members representing the Departments of State, Education, and Interior. Its Chairperson and Vice-Chairperson are also appointed by the President.

It was Elie Wiesel whose vision, initiative, and power of persuasion led to the establishment of the Commission and the Council. His spirit inspired not only the Commission's recommendations but also the very process of creating the Museum. Were it not for him, the Museum would not have come into existence.

According to the legislation passed by Congress, the federal government was authorized to provide land for the Museum, whereas the funds for its construction had to come from private donations.

The Museum was built on federal land, on Raoul Wallenberg Place in the heart of the capital. Standing on the Eisenhower Plaza, in front of the entrance to the

Museum, one can see the Washington Monument nearby on one's right, the Jefferson Memorial on one's left, with the Tidal Basin and the beautiful green lawns in between. The Museum is situated one block away from the National Mall, close to the Smithsonian Institution's group of national museums, yet separate enough to retain its uniqueness.

Over the years, an unusually successful fund-raising campaign provided the funds that made the creation of the Museum possible. From its inception, federal appropriations helped finance the educational and commemorative outreach activities that began long before the opening of the Museum, and currently federal appropriations cover a great part of its upkeep and operating budget.

The Commission's recommendation on Days of Remembrance was implemented as an integral part of the Museum's annual calendar. Every year since 1981, on Holocaust Remembrance Day, the Museum has organized a commemoration ceremony that usually takes place in the Rotunda of the Capitol. The ceremony culminates in the solemn lighting of six candles in memory of the millions of victims of the Holocaust.

The Commission also recommended establishing an educational foundation. However, rather than setting up a separate foundation, education became the central function of the Museum. Since the opening, the fund-raising campaign has been devoted mainly to the Museum's on-site and outreach educational activities.

According to another recommendation, a Committee on Conscience, composed of distinguished moral leaders in America, was to be established. The Committee would "receive reports of genocide (actual or potential) anywhere in the world. In the event of any outbreak it would have access to the President, the Congress, and the public in order to alert the national conscience, influence policy makers, and stimulate worldwide action to bring such acts to a halt . . . it would concentrate upon genocidal situations, transmitting information and advocating strong action on behalf of the United States, other countries, or the United Nations."

The recommendation left open many questions about the organizational framework and the appropriate parameters of the Committee's operation. After the Museum's opening, the Council found it appropriate to appoint an ad-hoc committee, composed of Council members, for the purpose of exploring the feasibility of such a Committee on Conscience.

As it was actually created under the leadership of the Council, the Museum represents the faithful implementation of the Commission's recommendations. It is stunning to see the high level of congruence, sometimes even in minor details, of the recommendations with the outcome.

The process of creating the Museum was led by a group of dedicated Council members who came to regard the Museum as the most important project of their lives. Among them were Harvey M. Meyerhoff, who in December 1986 replaced Elie Wiesel as Chairman of the Council; William J. Lowenberg, the Vice-Chairman; Albert Abramson, the Chairman of the Council's Museum Development Committee, in charge both of construction and of creation of the Museum's content; Miles Lerman, the present Council Chairman, who headed the successful fund-raising campaign and negotiated with the Soviet Union and virtually all other Eastern European countries the agreements that led to the acquisition of most of the artifacts for the Museum's Permanent Exhibition; and Benjamin Meed, the President of the American Gathering, the association of Jewish Holocaust survivors in the United States, who, together with Hadassa Rosensaft and other prominent members of the survivor community, enlisted the unwavering support of the survivors for the Museum.

These lay leaders would not have been able to accomplish their task were it not for the devoted and powerful assistance of Congressman Sidney Yates of Chicago who, from the beginning, identified with the project with all his heart. His spouse, Addie Yates, energetically spearheaded the effort to commemorate in the Museum the children who perished in the Holocaust.

In 1993, after the opening of the Museum, the Council resolved to adopt the following mission statement defining the tasks it should fulfill in society and the lines along which it should develop its activities.

The United States Holocaust Memorial Museum is America's national institution for the documentation, study, and interpretation of Holocaust history, and serves as this country's memorial to the millions of people murdered during the Holocaust.

The Holocaust was the state-sponsored, systematic persecution and annihilation of European Jewry by Nazi Germany and its collaborators between 1933 and 1945. Jews were the primary victims—six million were murdered; Gypsies, the handicapped, and Poles were also targeted for destruction or decimation for racial, ethnic or national reasons. Millions more, including homosexuals, Jehovah's Witnesses, Soviet prisoners of war and political dissidents, also suffered grievous oppression and death under Nazi tyranny.

The Museum's primary mission is to advance and disseminate knowledge about this unprecedented tragedy; to preserve the memory of those who suffered; and to encourage its visitors to reflect upon the moral and spiritual questions raised by the events of the Holocaust as well as their own responsibilities as citizens of a democracy.

Chartered by an unanimous Act of Congress in 1980 and located adjacent to the National Mall in Washington, D.C., the Museum strives to broaden public understanding of the history of the Holocaust through multi-faceted programs: exhibitions, research and publications; collecting and preserving material evidence, art and artifacts relating to the Holocaust; annual Holocaust commemoration days known as Days of Remembrance; distribution of educational material and teacher resources; and a variety of public programming designed to enhance understanding of the Holocaust and related issues, and including those of contemporary significance.

THE BUILDING

A RESONATOR OF MEMORY

For James Ingo Freed, the architect of the United States Holocaust Memorial Museum, the building is "a resonator of memory." Freed, who is a senior partner of Pei, Cobb, Freed & Partners in New York, escaped from Hitler's Germany as a child in 1939.

Towards the end of 1986, the Council approached Freed with the view to engage him as the architect of the building. This is how he describes the beginning of his involvement in the project.

> *The interview was promising, and I returned in high spirits, which slowly began to deflate when I realized how little I knew of the Holocaust. The Museum kindly forwarded video tapes, books, and articles, and night after night I would read and watch and become more and more morose as my ignorance gave way to a cruel history as seen through a rational glass. And I could not really start. Before saying that it was not going to work, I decided to take a trip to some of the killing grounds, and there in Auschwitz on my first night in the camp it all fell apart for me, and I began to cry, and a sort of angry passion shook me, and I knew I had to do this for those who were gone and who we must remember and for the survivors who knew, and for those like myself who did not know but knew we did not know and who, but for the accident of time, would have known. We owed the greatest debt, for we had not only survived but had survived in ignorance.*
>
> *Of course, such emotion cannot be sustained, but its meaning can, and that supported me through seven years of commitment. And it caused an internal reconstructing as well of my work in architecture. The emotion remains in the work.*
>
> *The drive to build this resonator of memory exhausted my store of known architectural strategies and left me to a constant search for the balanced joining of invention and memory. In short, I was free to search for meaning. What irony. (Milken Foundation Calendar)*

Sketch of the building by architect James Ingo Freed.

Facing page: Staircase in the Hall of Witness.

Entering the Museum, visitors find themselves enveloped in a very unusual atmosphere. This is for the visitors the transition space separating everyday reality from the ghost world of the Holocaust exhibition which they are about to see. It is a difficult border to cross. The monumental four-story atrium known as the Hall of Witness, which is the entrance hall of the building, evokes an immediate emotional reaction. People speak of feelings of fear, loneliness, helplessness, almost of panic, but also of holiness. Looking around, visitors realize that they are surrounded by red brick walls and dark-gray steel structures, reminiscent of a prison building. The hall's roof is an enormous skylight, whose glass-and-steel structures are skewed, a hint at the state of the world in Holocaust times. A wide stairway leads up to the second floor, ending in a brick gate whose arch is shaped exactly like the gate to the death camp of Auschwitz-Birkenau. This is not the only image brought by the architect from his visit to Auschwitz. The pattern of the bricks in the walls is reminiscent of the barracks in Auschwitz I. The northern side of the building is made up of a row of four interlinked brick structures, shaped like outsized Auschwitz watchtowers. However, even those who have never been in

Auschwitz can experience the atmospheric impact of the stern structural metaphors and elements used by the architect in the design of the building. The ambiance, although unfriendly, hard, and oppressive, grips visitors rather than drives them away. They face a similar ambivalence when finding themselves, at last, in the exhibition.

Whether consciously or unconsciously, Freed has designed what could be regarded as a self-sufficient memorial monument to the victims of the Holocaust. The building would have been an outstanding architectural statement even if it had not contained a historical museum. It affords visitors an experience similar to that experienced by a believer in a holy place. Like a cathedral, the Hall of Witness is awe-inspiring, overwhelming in its monumentality, making the individual feel small and insignificant. One is, indeed, tempted to ask whether the building needs a museum at all, since it has reached a level of architectural perfection that would sustain it as a unique memorial, even without the addition of any exhibition materials.

On the second floor of the building the architect has created the Hall of Remembrance, an impressive, large hexagonal space, brightly lit during the daytime by its skylight. As its entrance directly faces the exit from the Permanent Exhibition, visitors feel invited, on completion of their walk-through, to enter the serene hall and pause, perhaps for some minutes of contemplation, before returning to the real world. The Hall of Remembrance, with its Eternal Flame, is designed to serve the Museum as formal memorial space. Here commemoration ceremonies are held for Jewish and non-Jewish victims of the Holocaust, here people say Kaddish (the Jewish prayer of commemoration), here they can light candles in memory of relatives and friends who perished in the Holocaust. The walls are inscribed with the names of the twenty most important concentration and death camps. Whereas the Hall of Witness is always busy, the Hall of Remembrance is quiet. One is somber, the other full of very bright light—almost too bright for mourning, perhaps conveying the sense of hope. As the building's two architectural focal points, they form aesthetic and atmospheric counterpoints.

Commemoration ceremony in the Hall of Remembrance.

The building as memorial is complemented by the museum exhibition, the visual narrative of the commemorated event. Generally speaking, monuments have memorial validity only for people who are familiar with the commemorated personality or event. The memorial in the death camp of Treblinka, for instance, is one of the strongest of its kind. One is overwhelmed by the sight of 17,000 granite stones of different shapes and sizes that symbolically represent the communities of the Jewish victims who were murdered in the camp. However, for those who never heard that hundreds of thousands of victims were killed in this death camp, the memorial, with all its aesthetic strength and emotional impact, has no meaning. It may as well be a piece of environmental art onto which each viewer can project his own individual interpretation. It will remain a memorial only for those who know. Fifty years hence, Freed's building will retain its aesthetic power as a work of great architectural art even without the exhibition and the institutional activities of the Museum. But if it were not for the exhibition, by then only a few would know this chapter of history.

In the United States Holocaust Memorial Museum, the building and the exhibition work in tandem. The memorial building envelops the exhibition with the right ambiance; the exhibition endows the memorial building with historical context. Moreover, Freed created a circulation path in the building, leading from the Hall of Witness, through the main exhibition spaces, the bridges, the watchtower rooms, the lounges, to the other monumental hall, the hexagonal Hall of Remembrance. From here the path leads back to the Hall of Witness. The circulation path of the building intertwines harmonically with that of the exhibition. Both circle around the Hall of Witness, which is the central space of the building and which can be viewed by the visitor at various points of this combined path. Thus a continual discourse is taking place between building and exhibition.

However, not in all respects was this discourse without its challenges. Since the building design was virtually completed before the design process of the exhibition had even started, exhibition design had to adapt itself to the given architectural contours.

The skylight over the Hall of Witness seen through glass etched with the names of lost communities.

From the planners' point of view, for example, the glass bridges leading from the main exhibition spaces of the watchtower rooms created an interruption in the exhibition flow. They feared that the bridges might dissipate the emotional impact of the exhibition on visitors. They eventually found a creative solution for their integration. On alternate floors, the glass walls of the bridges are covered with names of perished Jewish communities and first names of Holocaust victims. The bridges were transformed into much-needed breathing spaces for visitors bombarded with painful images and information. For the same reason, the planners decided that the pie-shaped lounges that lead to the stairways from one exhibition floor to the other should not contain any images relating to the Holocaust. They serve as "neutral" places of rest and contemplation.

Another architectural challenge lay in the watchtower rooms. By designing one whole side of the building as a row of gigantic watchtowers, the architect created on each floor a sequence of four interlinked square spaces that the visitor has to walk through in order to get from one exhibition level to the other. Whereas in the main spaces the planners were free to design the exhibition according to the inherent logic of the story line, here they were forced to adapt themselves on each floor to design constraints imposed by the shape and location of the four tower rooms. In this case, not all design solutions were satisfactory. However, one of them was superb. One of the towers was used to accommodate an exhibit with more than a thousand photographs, which came to be called the "Tower of Faces." For this, the architect created an actual three-story tower inside one of the symbolic watchtowers. Thus collaboration of architectural with exhibition design led to the creation of one of the most touching and impressive components of the Permanent Exhibition, which several reviewers have called "the heart of the building."

Whereas it seems that the architect had conceived the building as a monument, the planners wanted it also to become the container of a living organism consisting collectively of the many people who would come to the Museum to see, to experience, to absorb, to learn, and to undergo change. As a memorial rather than a museum, the building is understandably unkind and unwelcoming, not necessarily caring for the needs of the visiting public. As with the design of a freestanding memorial, no restaurant or cafeteria were included in the Museum's design for fear of desecrating the holiness of the place. This design also lacked necessary

office space for museum staff, which grew to more than 300 employees. And there was too little space for the other operational needs of the Museum such as for storage, workshops, and the like.

Although architecture as a discipline belongs essentially to the domain of aesthetics, it always serves functional purposes defined by the client. Normally, architects strive to optimize in their design both aesthetics and function. The concept of this museum building, however, entailed a certain tension between the function of a memorial and the function of a museum.

This tension between the function of a memorial and that of a museum was never totally resolved, but most of the practical difficulties were eventually remedied. Sometime after construction began, the Museum obtained an old, unused, two-story federal office building adjacent to the construction site. Though early on it was hoped that the building could be demolished to give the Museum and its plaza a sight line to the Washington Monument, it was a landmark and gaining permission to destroy it would have been difficult. Instead, the Museum restored its impressive facade but adapted its interior to the needs of the Museum. It today provides the space for a modest cafeteria as well as Museum administration offices.

Today, the Museum is proud of the outstanding architectural creation that shapes the right emotional frame of mind for the visitor. The building constitutes one of the two main pillars of the Museum's success, the other being the Permanent Exhibition.

ART IN PUBLIC SPACES

One of the basic design decisions was to not include artistic creations in the Permanent Exhibition. Among other considerations, the decision was guided by the commitment that all exhibits should be of authentic documentary character in order to preempt attempts by those who would deny that the Holocaust took place from using the Museum as supporting evidence for Holocaust denial. The exhibition planners also wanted to avoid any softening in the depiction of the stark reality of the Holocaust by the inclusion of symbolic or metaphoric exhibits, any blurring of the terrible truth by sublimation.

This restriction, however, did not apply to the public spaces in the building. The Museum established an "Art for Public Spaces" program and commissioned four works of art, each of which was to be created in direct response to its respective site. The artists were chosen by an independent jury composed of distinguished art experts from around the country. The commissioned works were intended to be distinct from the narrative and documentary character of the Museum's permanent historical exhibition. They were created by eminent contemporary American artists: Ellsworth Kelly, Sol LeWitt, Richard Serra, and Joel Shapiro.

The art in the Museum's public spaces is conceived as complementing the architecture. It is

Facing page: Joel Shapiro's *Loss and Regeneration*, situated on Eisenhower Plaza.

Ellsworth Kelly's *Memorial* is composed of four white wall sculptures on two facing walls.

integrated in the architectural circulation path created by Freed rather than in the circulation path of the Permanent Exhibition.

Ellsworth Kelly's and Sol LeWitt's works were created for the two pie-shaped lounges linking the fourth with the third floor and the third with the second floor. These lounges, rather than merging with the flow of the exhibition, were intended to create a pause in the flow for rest and contemplation. Figurative creations relating to the Holocaust would not permit the intended breathing spell, whereas figurative art not relating to the Holocaust would introduce distracting alien themes. Therefore the art had to be abstract.

Ellsworth Kelly's *Memorial,* in the third-floor lounge, consists of four wall-mounted flat panels (called by the artist "wall sculptures"). Three of the panels are of identical rectangular shapes, and mounted in an even sequence. The fourth, much larger than the others, is fan shaped and mounted on the opposite wall. All four are entirely white, just like the walls on which they are mounted. They become an integral part of the environment, determining the ambiance of the lounge. Kelly has likened the sequence of the three rectangular panels to memorial tablets that, in their anonymity, bear the names of all victims of the Holocaust.

Sol LeWitt's *Consequence,* in the second-floor lounge, is a wall painting, made by applying ink to the wall. It entirely covers the large wall of the room with five equal squares, each consisting of squares-within-squares and surrounded by a black frame. The central square is gray, circumscribed by a band of white. The large area between black outer frame and central gray square is distinctly colored, the chromatic range from square to square being the result of different combinations of either red, yellow, blue, or gray. An art critic commented on Sol LeWitt's work that it "may seem a form of tomb painting, appropriately enough given that you've just come from the part of the Permanent Exhibition that describes the death camps. . . . But if this work evokes mourning, it also, like Kelly's, offers the consolation of purified aesthetic experience." (Ken Johnson in *Art and Memory,* November 1993)

Richard Serra's *Gravity* divides the lower steps of the stairway leading from the Hall of Witness to the Concourse level.

In contrast to the works of Kelly and LeWitt, Richard Serra's and Joel Shapiro's sculptures are positioned in very public locations, outside the circulation path of the exhibition. Richard Serra's piece can be seen on the landing of the stairway leading from the Hall of Witness down to the Concourse level of the building. Shapiro's two-part sculpture was placed outside the building, on the Eisenhower Plaza, in front of the western entrance to the Museum. Both have become integral components of building's architecture.

Serra's *Gravity* is a large square slab of unpolished steel wedged into the stairs at the foot of the black granite wall that covers the west side of the Hall of Witness. It looks threatening and malevolent, and thus adds to the heavy, disquieting atmosphere of the Hall of Witness. Initially Serra was invited by the architect to assist him in shaping a large vertical crack in the granite wall, which was to symbolize the rupture in human society caused by the Holocaust. But in the ensuing dialogue between architect and artist, the idea of the crack was abandoned, and the concept of the sculpture adopted instead.

Shapiro's bronze sculpture *Loss and Regeneration* consists of two separate parts, located on two different levels of the plaza, at some distance from each other. One clearly represents a house standing upside down on its roof; it could metaphorically represent upheaval in human life, in the life of the family. The other is a tall, abstract, distorted figure, which can be viewed as a tree or a human being, perhaps as a truncated family tree or a person in distress. A dialogue seems to be going on between the two. Shapiro's sculpture, dedicated to the children who perished in the Holocaust, is the most figurative of the four works of art in the Museum. Its plaque carries the following lines written by a child in the Terezin ghetto: "Until, after a long time, I'd be well again. / Then I'd like to live /And go back home again."

Whereas the building's atmosphere is disquieting, and the exhibition depicts the most horrible aspects of human character, the art in the Museum, like all art, comes out of the goodness of human creativity. Thus the art represents an attempt to introduce a small, soothing, comforting element into the painful Museum visit.

Sol LeWitt's *Consequence.*

Below and facing page: Entrance to the building
from 14th Street.

Overleaf: In the Hall of Witness.

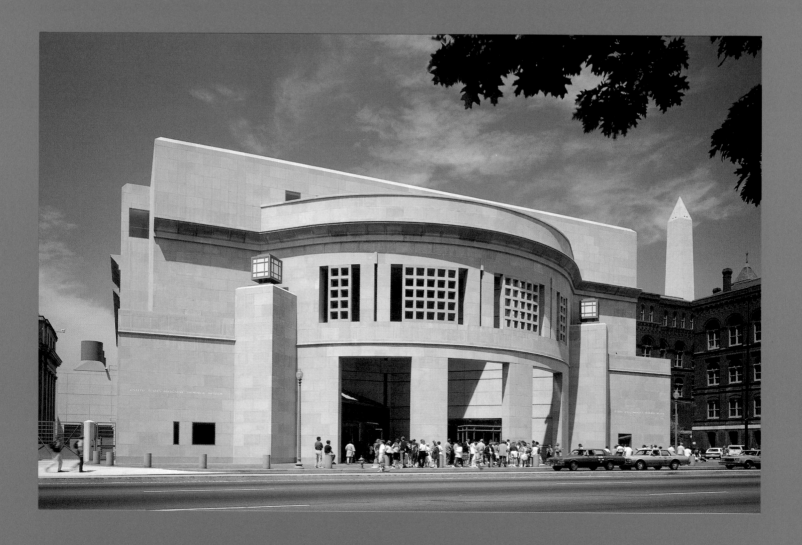

The Hall of Witness.

Window in the Hall of Witness.

Facing page: Concourse level showing connection to the Hall of Witness, and on left part of the Childrens' Tile Wall.

Facing page: Glass bridge.

Below: Concourse level.

The Hall of Remembrance.

Facing page: Ground floor adjacent to the Hall of Witness.

Above: Joseph and Rebecca Meyerhoff Theater.

Overleaf: The Museum and the Eisenhower Plaza.

THE EXHIBITION

A NARRATIVE MUSEUM

The United States Holocaust Memorial Museum is a *narrative* historical museum. Unlike most historical museums, it is based on a narrative rather than on a collection of works of art and artifacts relating to history.

Traditional historical museums consider it their main concern to collect and preserve, research and publicly display authentic objects belonging to their specific fields of interest. By doing so, these museums render a service of greatest importance: their collections permit direct access to evidence from primary sources, which is tantamount to preserving knowledge. But though they may be receptacles of knowledge, such museums usually do not educate in the sense of changing and developing their visitors mentally, emotionally, or morally. In most cases, they mainly convey information and aesthetic impressions.

The narrative history museum, on the other hand, has strong educational potential. It uses its exhibits as building blocks in a continuous story line and displays them in their historical context. A well-constructed narrative exhibition affects visitors not only intellectually but also emotionally; it arouses processes of identification. Visitors project themselves into the story and thus experience it like insiders while at the same time remaining at a distance, with the intellectual perspective of outsiders.

The narrative museum goes beyond displaying collected items. It is based on the premise that exhibits have to be presented in a context that allows their full significance to be understood and appreciated. The narrative continuum is as important as the objects themselves. Drawn into the flow of the narrative, visitors view the display with their senses tuned to sequence, coherence, and transformation. They not only register isolated facts, they also search for meaning. They walk through the exhibition galleries as if walking through a three-dimensionally presented oral history whose meaning transcends the original historical limitations of time and space.

Comprehension of the narrative and its meaning is not only an intellectual but also an emotional experience. The emotional effect of the narrative in the museum exhibition is comparable to that of the narrative in novels, plays, or motion pictures. All of them are based on plot. The plot triggers identification, which envelops us mentally and forces us to relate to the meaning of the story line. What would we have done had we been in the given situations, we ask ourselves. Just as we do when reading a novel or viewing a theater performance or a feature film, we identify with the protagonists. Being gripped by the plot, projecting ourselves into it, identifying with its heroes and developing resentment towards its villains, we get emotionally involved. This emotional involvement opens us to educational influence.

All this is well known and has been applied many times in different fields for the purpose of education. Why had it hardly ever been applied in the framework of museums?

Top: The beginning of the Exhibition.

Bottom: Viewing prisoner identification photographs made at Auschwitz.

Facing page: Visitors viewing images of medical experiments at Auschwitz.

The reason seems to lie in the way museums developed historically. Museums originated with princely collections of treasures and rarities that aroused the curiosity of viewers and impressed them with the wealth and importance of the owner. "To show the collection" was the original purpose of museums; it remained until very recently the main purpose of most exhibitions. They did not pretend to educate.

Not until after World War II did the museum world abolish its traditional rigid adherence to collection-based display patterns and open up to a great variety of different approaches. Modern science and children's museums were established whose point of departure were the messages they wanted to convey rather than the collections they called their own. These museums undertook to offer visitors information, concepts, and ideas rather than to show valuable or interesting objects isolated from environmental or historical context. These museums were essentially teaching instruments, and in pursuit of their didactic goal they created or commissioned the creation of exhibits to communicate the desired message.

The world-famous Exploratorium in San Francisco is perhaps the best example of a museum that embraced a radical educational approach. All its exhibits are custom-tailored teaching devices. Moreover, it is a "hands-on" museum—the visitors are invited to use the devices to actively explore basic aspects of the physical world. The exhibits have no historical value, they are not authentic. Thus the Exploratorium sacrificed the most sacred taboo of the traditional museum world—namely, the principle of authenticity—on the altar of didactic expediency. So did many modern science and children's museums.

However, the Exploratorium and most other generically related teaching-oriented science museums do not consider it their task to affect and change the mental and moral attitudes of their visitors. The United States Holocaust Memorial Museum does. To do so, it had to adopt the narrative approach. Like the science museums, it disseminates knowledge. It is communication-based rather than collection-based. But it goes one step further: it tries to communicate a historical narrative. Thanks to the plot-based narrative embodied in its exhibits, it is endowed with an educational power likely to act on mental attitudes and behavior patterns. Thus it was perhaps the ultimate compliment when, in a thoughtful article about the Holocaust Museum published immediately after its opening, Leon Wieseltier, the literary editor of *The New Republic,* called it "a pedagogical masterpiece."

The first history museum consistently based on the narrative approach was created in Israel. When Beth Hatefutsoth, the Nahum Goldmann Museum of the Jewish Diaspora, opened in Tel Aviv in 1978, it succeeded in pulling together into one continuous narrative the usually fragmented knowledge about the various well-known milestones in Jewish history. It was exceedingly well accepted by the public. Many visitors found there for the first time answers to their questions about the overall context of two millennia of Jewish Diaspora history. Suddenly the many unconnected fragments they remembered from childhood fell into place. Individuals placed themselves within the historical continuum; they could identify intellectually and emotionally with their people. Despite its public success, the Israeli Association of Museums hesitated for quite some time to accept the Diaspora Museum as a member institution. The reason given for the initial hesitation was that it did not have a collection of its own.

In the meantime, various other narrative history museums opened in Israel, the United States, and other countries. The United States Holocaust Memorial Museum is one of them and can be regarded as a methodological offspring of the Diaspora Museum in Tel Aviv.

A narrative history museum is different from a collecting museum in many of its fundamental characteristics. One of the most important of these is the imposition of a certain necessary sequence on the arrangement of the exhibits. The sequence is determined by the flow of the narrative the museum intends to present and any deviation from it affects the content of that narrative. Moreover, since the containing structures that hold the three-dimensional exhibits are physically integrated in the continuum of the narrative presentation, changes in the composition of the exhibition are more often than not liable to necessitate costly changes in these structures. Thus, once it is installed, a narrative museum has a relatively high level of resistance to any change in the choice and arrangement of its three-dimensional exhibits.

The curators are the backbone of collecting museums. Curators are academicians with specialized knowledge about the subject matter of the collection they oversee. They conduct research on the objects in the collection, they administer it and enhance it by new acquisitions, and they display some of it to the public. The narrative history museum, in contrast, does not use collection curators for the creation of its permanent exhibition. It is the historian, rather than the curator, who has to provide the necessary academic expertise that relates to the historical period covered by the narrative rather than to any specific category of exhibits or collection of objects.

By leading visitors through a narrative, the museum forces them to follow a preconceived circulation path. The visitors are not free to choose their own way through the museum, just as they are not free to choose their own way between the scenes of a play or a film. This restriction, usually not imposed in collection-based museums or art galleries, is the price that has to be paid for having the museum exhibition based on a narrative.

The planning team at work. From left to right:
Ralph Appelbaum, the designer;
Raye Farr, Exhibition Department Director;
Jeshajahu Weinberg, Museum Director.

It is customary for museums and exhibitions to list and describe their exhibits in a catalogue. In a narrative history museum, a descriptive list of exhibits is essentially pointless, because the individual exhibits derive their meaning and significance from their position in the historical context. Visitors would not be helped by a traditional annotated catalogue in their efforts to understand the meaning of the exhibits.

Surely, the narrative approach is not of exclusive validity, not even in the domain of history museums. But it is probably one of the best ways for history museums to realize their educational potential. It is the approach the United States Holocaust Memorial Museum chose to adopt.

THE PLANNING TEAM

The foundation for the five-year-long design process was the decision to base the Permanent Exhibition of the United States Holocaust Memorial Museum on the narrative concept. This affected the composition of the design team, the research, and the goals of the exhibit-collecting effort. This narrative concept also determined the way the exhibition design would interact with the building.

In collection-based museums, exhibition design is traditionally the result of a tug-of-war between a curator, who represents content, and an exhibition designer, who represents form. The two, often equally strong agents, give birth to the exhibition through

Above: Ralph Appelbaum, designer of the exhibition (left), and Martin Smith, the first Exhibition Department Director.

incessant discourse. A narrative museum, in contrast, needs the expertise of historians, not curators. It also needs a designer with experience in the conceptual design of narrative historical exhibitions and a thorough mastery of the historical subject matter. Design is not the imposition of form, but a tool to present the narrative story line.

In view of these considerations, the Museum Director decided to build a design team composed of museum staff organized as an Exhibition Department. Instead of hiring a designer as a leader of the team, an outside designer was brought in as a member of the team. This gave the client—that is, the Director—not just approval rights but full operational control over the process in all its stages while still allowing the exhibit to benefit from the talent and technical skill of an experienced design expert.

Working under the guidance of the Museum Director, the head of the Exhibition Department had to be able to cope with problems of both content and form and with the synthesis of the two in the visually presented narrative. At first, it seemed to be difficult to find the right candidate for the position of department director, since it was not clear in what professional discipline one could hope to find the needed qualifications. The search for a qualified candidate did not exclude museum personnel and exhibition designers, but eventually, after lengthy consultations, it was decided to offer the position to an English film director with experience in the production of modern historical documentaries.

The presentation of Martin Smith's film "The Struggles of Poland" on public television led to his selection as Exhibition Department Director. At first Smith was utterly surprised by the unexpected and unusual offer, but soon he became persuaded that it would be an interesting challenge for him to create an historical narrative as an exhibition, in three-dimensional museum space, rather than as a motion picture on a two-dimensional television screen. He agreed to come to Washington for two years, and it proved to be a most fortunate choice. His contribution to the shaping of the Permanent Exhibition was invaluable. After two years he returned to London and the position of Exhibition Department Director was given to another outstanding film professional, Raye Farr, who also came from the world of historical documentaries. She, too, made an important contribution to the creation of the Permanent Exhibition. When the Museum opened, Raye Farr chose to join the permanent Museum staff as the head of the Film and Video Department.

A detailed model of the exhibition helped planners during the design process.

The project still needed the input of a highly qualified museum designer with ample experience in the design of displays and with the backup of professional staff as well as technical facilities. The contract was offered to, and accepted by, Ralph Appelbaum, a well-known designer based in New York. Appelbaum became an effective team player, and, like Smith, made a major creative contribution to the design process and to the success of the exhibition. The aesthetics of the exhibition bear witness to his great talent.

The exhibition planning team was thus composed of the Museum Director, Jeshajahu Weinberg, the proponent of the narrative approach, who acted as the overall orchestrator of the planning process; the Exhibition Department Director, Martin Smith, later followed by Raye Farr; the designer, Ralph Appelbaum; and the representative of content, Michael Berenbaum, an expert on Holocaust history who later became the Director of the Museum's Holocaust Research Institute. Berenbaum, who had temporarily been a member of the Museum staff in the days of the President's Commission, not only made an extraordinary contribution to the shaping of the exhibition's content, but also fulfilled a most important role as convincing spokesman for the entire institution.

This core team was supported and supplemented by a large group of dedicated and competent professionals who were involved in the writing and editing of the exhibition's textual elements, in the acquisition and care of artifacts, in photo research, and in the production of maps, audiovisual programs, and films.

For the sake of methodological clarity, the planners divided the design process into three major phases: Conceptual design, macro-design and micro-design. In the conceptual design phase, the exhibition's story-line and its overall structure were determined. In the macro-design phase, the story-line was embedded in the building, thus creating the basic circulation path. At the same time, a world-wide hunt was conducted for potential exhibits—artifacts, photographs and moving pictures. In the micro-design phase, the individual exhibits were chosen and integrated in display segments. The actual production of audio-visual programs also was carried out in this phase.

In reality, the three phases were partially overlapping, since the design process entailed an ongoing rethinking of the story line. Such rethinking was sometimes made necessary when an important artifact unexpectedly turned out to be available or, conversely, unavailable.

CONCEPTUAL DESIGN

Although the point of departure for the conceptual design was the decision to build the exhibition along a narrative course, the actual history of the Holocaust

could never be identical with a single story line. Every narrative is an interpretation by the storyteller, and in this case the interpretation had to be twofold: a basic, historiographical retelling and a design-oriented one.

The general outlines of the historical interpretation were implicitly agreed among the planners. But a major difficulty was encountered in extracting an appropriate visual story line from the overwhelming multitude and magnitude of the historical event of the Holocaust. The visual component had to represent the nonlinear historical reality of the subject matter, yet also correspond to the linear circulation path of the visitor.

The opening segment of each of the three exhibition floors.

Three structural choices for the exhibition seemed available: the structure could be based on a linear chronological sequence; on geography, relating the story country by country rather than year by year; or on a linear sequence of major themes inherent in the story of the Holocaust. None of these basic choices, by themselves, was able to provide a satisfactory overall solution.

These different approaches were combined to provide the desired structural framework for the exhibition. The result was complex but extremely well suited to the multifaceted character of the story line. The period from 1933 until the beginning of the Second World War in 1939 lent itself to a linear, chronological sequence. But once the Holocaust began to spread throughout occupied Europe, the chronological structure became inadequate. At any given point in time, different events took place in the various countries conquered by Nazi Germany. Adherence to sequence in time would have required a synchronous presentation, which was not possible within a linear museum walk-through. A presentation by country, on the other hand, would have been utterly repetitive. It would have implied telling the same story again and again, because the implementation of the "Final Solution" of the Nazis unfolded in most countries along the same basic lines.

To overcome these difficulties, the planning team chose a sequential structure for the second part of the Permanent Exhibition that was based on an analysis of the recurring main stages of the "Final Solution": ghettos, deportations, concentration camps, death camps. In its final part, the exhibition returns to the linear, chronological structure. This was possible because the final stages of the Holocaust—the death marches, the liberation and the "aftermath" (the war crime trials, the Holocaust refugee camps, etc.)—occurred more or less simultaneously in different countries.

In the final part, the visitor also finds three thematic exhibition sections outside the historic sequence. They are devoted to the rescue of Jews by non-Jews during the Holocaust, to resistance against the perpetrators, and to the fate of children in the Holocaust. The episodes presented in these sections are grouped together by theme, irrespective of time or location.

Among members of the planning team, the most controversial issue was the inclusion of thematic sections on rescue and resistance. Some members of the planning team felt that rescue and resistance were quantitatively marginal phenomena in the Holocaust, and that devoting separate thematic sections to them toward the end of the exhibition would distort the historical truth by inserting into the story line an unwarranted, massive upbeat element. They believed that episodes of rescue and resistance should be presented in the immediate historic context in which they occurred. Others thought that the episodes of rescue and resistance were of great enough educational importance to warrant separate thematic treatment. They argued that rescuers should be regarded as role models for people who find themselves in the position of bystanders, whereas resisters should be regarded as role models for victimized population groups. The latter argument prevailed.

There may be some truth in the argument that the legendary story of Raoul Wallenberg, the daring Swedish diplomat who saved thousands of Jews in Budapest, or that of Oscar Schindler who saved over a thousand Jews from certain death in the gas chambers, are loaded with mythical overtones. The same can probably be said about the Warsaw ghetto uprising, about Anna Frank, and about the Palestinian Jewish poet Hanna Senesh, who parachuted behind the enemy lines and was executed in Hungary. It is an open question whether educational considerations justify the Museum's decision to perpetuate these legends by presenting them in the exhibition in such a prominent fashion, even though this presentation restricts itself meticulously to the undisputed underlying historic facts.

It was not easy to decide how to end the exhibition. Albert Abramson, one of the Museum's most influential, leading Council members without whom the Museum would never have happened, strongly opposed an ending without hope. In his opinion, it would be a mistake to conclude the Museum visit on an utterly depressive note. He wanted the Museum visitors to take away with them a strong message of belief in the future, in education, in the possibility of change. The planning team was united in its opposition to any upbeat ending, considering it a distortion of historical truth. In the final design decision, the two seemingly contradictory approaches were reconciled and synthesized. A film composed of fragments of Holocaust survivors' testimonies became the last exhibit in the circulation path. The selection of these fragments focused on episodes of rescue and of both armed and spiritual resistance. In these episodes, the film shows pain, suffering, and anguish, but also resilience, compassion, and hope. The planning team understood that a comprehensive picture of the Holocaust with all its horror and darkness must also include these manifestations of humane behavior.

The exhibition segment devoted to the story of Raoul Wallenberg.

THE CIRCULATION PATH

In the phase of macro-design, the story line was embedded in the building and thus it ceased to be an abstract concept. Ideally, the story line and its container, the building, would have been shaped in one combined, interactive design process, complementing each other. In this case, the building was designed before the exhibition and the story line had to be adapted to the architectural facts. The use of the tower rooms, for instance, was shaped by the given architecture. On the other hand, in some cases the architect did make minor changes in the building design

to accommodate large exhibits like the railway car, the Auschwitz barracks, and the "Tower of Faces." In spite of the inevitable problems of mutual adaption, the building succeeded in becoming an ideal companion to the exhibition.

The circulation path, which in the phase of conceptual planning was as abstract as the story line, now together with the story line assumed physical reality. Essentially the circulation path is an alter ego of the story line. But contrary to the story line it determines the sequence of exhibit elements as well as the actual, physical path of the visitor through the exhibition spaces.

When planning the circulation path during the macro-design phase, the team had to bring together three factors: the story line, the building, and the needs of

Installation of the Polish railway car during construction.

Below: Inside the elevator leading to the Permanent Exhibition a video presentation begins the exhibition.

the visiting public. Interaction among the three would determine the visitor's museum experience.

The team had to look at the path through the eyes of the public. Various considerations had to be taken into account. Some related to the physical comfort of visitors. Bottlenecks in the flow of visitors had to be prevented to enable them to come close to the exhibits and view them at their leisure. Providing benches and other resting opportunities was crucial, especially for the physically impaired and the elderly. There had to be easy access to water and to restrooms. Elevators had to be in place to carry the visitors from the Hall of Witness to the upper exhibition floor as well as to carry the physically impaired from one exhibition level to the other. And last but not least, visitors had to have the choice at various points of the circulation path to abandon the exhibition, if for whatever reason they felt that they could not continue. The care for the visitors' physical comfort was particularly important in view of the enormous stress they would be under when confronted with the difficult subject matter, the length of time needed to see the entire exhibition, and the physical distance that had to be covered.

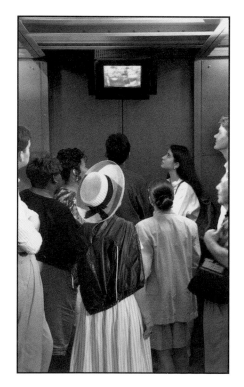

The actual circulation path in the Museum is certainly not flawless from the point of view of the visitors' comfort. Partly because of limitations given by the building itself and partly because of miscalculations made by the team regarding the number of daily visitors, not all potential problems found satisfactory solutions. The most severe were bottlenecks that seriously hampered the flow of visitors in two or three places. Even a year after the opening, structural changes were still under way to improve the circulation of the enormous crowds who daily entered the exhibition galleries.

The planning of the circulation path also had to take into account psychological factors. One of those was the transition visitors made from the outside reality into the building and the exhibition. In view of the serious shock inevitably caused by the encounter with the world of the Holocaust, the planning team had to find ways to ease the visitors into the exhibition. Only cautious pacing of the initial phases of the exhibition could prevent immediate rejection and instead elicit interest in the subject matter. To this end, introductory monitors were installed in the elevators lifting the visitors to the upper exhibition floor, and throughout the whole first floor circulation was slowed down by films presented in small sit-down theaters and by an abundance of information. The upper exhibition floor is, indeed, a preface to the actual presentation of the Holocaust.

No less important was the problem of how to protect the visitors, and mainly the children, from horrific images which they might not be able to cope with psychologically. Avoiding altogether the presentation of images of mass executions, corpses, gruesome medical experiments, etc. was impossible, because it would have been tantamount to sanitizing the Holocaust by the extraction of important elements from the story line. A solution was found in the construction of protection walls in front of monitors carrying the most problematic images. Visitors can decide whether to look behind these walls or to avoid the exhibits. Adults can make this choice on behalf of children. The walls were designed to prevent children of eight or nine years of age from casually seeing these pictures as they walked through the Permanent Exhibition.

Protective walls shield monitors that present images of attrocities.

The segments of the exhibition as well as their themes, positions, and sequence were also defined in this phase of design. The term "segment" was used by the planners to refer to thematic groupings of exhibits. The sequence of segments represented the story line in an intermediate stage between abstract concept and three-dimensional reality. For example, the exhibition begins with a segment describing the encounter of the victorious American army with the concentration camps, followed by segments on Jewish life before the Holocaust, the takeover of power in Germany by the Nazis in 1933, the beginning of Nazi terror, the boycott against Jewish shops in April 1933, the burning of books, the Nazi propaganda, the "science" of race, and so on. Only in the micro-design phase were the individual exhibits for each of the segments chosen.

SEARCH FOR EXHIBITS

Concurrent with its work on the sequence of exhibition segments, the planning team conducted a worldwide search for artifacts, photographs, and film footage. Staff members were sent to the Soviet Union and all other Eastern European Communist countries, and to Germany, Holland, and France. The search also covered Israel and the United States.

The search was informed by the decision that the exhibition should include only authentic material. The major reason for this decision lay in the recent upsurge in the activities of Holocaust deniers. Using authentic artifacts and photographs, the Museum itself would constitute historical evidence of the Holocaust.

The team deviated from the principle of authenticity in very few cases. Some large objects whose inclusion in the Museum was considered of great importance could not be brought to Washington. A team of specialists from England was sent to Poland and Austria to prepare fiberglass castings taken from the last remaining fragment of the Warsaw ghetto wall, the infamous inscription "Arbeit Macht Frei" ("Work Brings Freedom") from the gate of the Auschwitz death camp, the door to a gas chamber in the Majdanek death camp, the front of a crematorium in Mauthausen, the largest concentration camp in Austria, and more. The original objects, from which the fiberglass replicas were prepared, can still be inspected in situ by any who doubt they exist.

The team also commissioned the Polish sculptor Jan Stobierski to create a scale model of one of the Auschwitz gas chambers. Years before, he had created a similar model for display in the Auschwitz site museum. This model and the few fiberglass replicas were the only exceptions to the rule of including only authentic artifacts.

Top to bottom: Zyclon B poison crystals of the type used in the gas chambers; instruments used for identification of "race characteristics"; punch card tabulator used in Nazi population census.

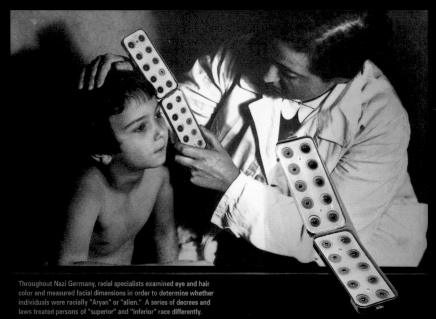

Throughout Nazi Germany, racial specialists examined eye and hair color and measured facial dimensions in order to determine whether individuals were racially "Aryan" or "alien." A series of decrees and laws treated persons of "superior" and "inferior" race differently.

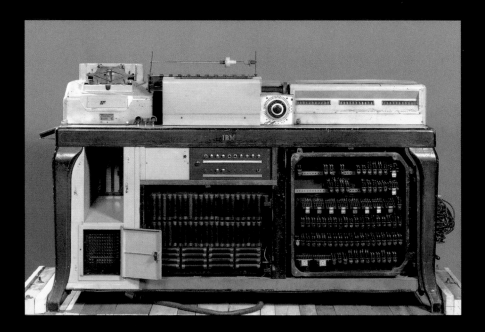

Статья 9

Это Соглашение будет действовать в течение пяти лет и может быть продлено на следующие пять лет по согласию обеих сторон. Действие Соглашения может быть прекращено через шесть месяцев после письменного извещения одной из сторон другой о своем желании провести новые переговоры, внести изменения или прекратить действие Соглашения.

Это Соглашение подписано в г.Москве 12 июня 1989 г. в двух экземплярах, на русском и английском языках, оба текста являются идентичными.

За Главное архивное управление при Совете Министров СССР

Ф.М.Ваганов

За Американский Совет памяти нацизма /Холокост/

М.Лерман

Signature page of agreement between the Museum and the main archival administration in Soviet Russia.

A major breakthrough in the search for exhibit material was achieved when Miles Lerman, then Chairman of the Museum's Committee on International Relations and currently Chairman of the United States Holocaust Memorial Council, succeeded in signing formal agreements with the government of virtually every Eastern European Communist country. As a federal agency, the Museum signed the agreements on behalf of the United States, as it were, after their wording had been checked and approved by the State Department. They were all revalidated by the successor governments after the breakdown of the Communist regimes in Eastern Europe.

These agreements granted the Museum access to many Eastern European Holocaust-related site museums and archives. They enabled members of the Museum staff to microfilm countless Holocaust-related documents and to bring to Washington thousands of artifacts which were to become the mainstay of the exhibition. Many of the artifacts came from the site museums of Auschwitz and Majdanek. Others came from the Jewish Historical Institute in Warsaw and from the Main Commission for the Investigation of War Crimes in Warsaw, from museums in Vilnius, the capital of Lithuania, in Banska Bistriza (Slovakia), and elsewhere. Among these artifacts were four thousand shoes of victims who were gassed in Majdanek, a barracks from Auschwitz, prisoners' bunks from Majdanek, and a railway car of the kind that was used to carry victims from the Warsaw ghetto to the gas chamber of Treblinka.

As the result of the search and the survivors' donations, many extraordinary items were brought to Washington: Torah scrolls from Germany and Austria desecrated by the Nazis during the nationwide pogrom in November 1938 known as the "Kristallnacht"; posters with announcements by German authorities and ghetto administrations; the milk can that was found after the war in the rubble of ghetto Warsaw, full of important historical documents on life in the ghetto; cobblestones from a street in ghetto Warsaw; striped inmate uniforms from concentration camps; fence posts from Auschwitz; a Danish fisherman's boat that was used to carry 900 Jews to safety in Sweden; children's toys from ghettos and camps; and weapons of Jewish resistance fighters in Eastern and Western Europe, and many other items.

Notice by Jewish Council in Ghetto Radom warning residents of punishment for failure to report for labor service.

WARNUNG
an die jüdische Bevölkerung.

Auf Anordnung des Arbeitsamtes Radom geben wir bekannt, dass von jetzt an gegen diejenigen, die der Aufforderung des ARBEITSAMTES zur Arbeitsstellung oder zur Registration nicht pünktlich Folge leisten, die schärfsten Strafen, Gefängnis oder Konzentrationslager, angesetzt werden.

Angesichts dessen fordern wir die gestellungspflichtigen Juden nochmals auf, alle Anweisungen des Arbeitsamtes UNBEDINGT an den festgesetzten Terminen zu befolgen.

Radom, den 18. Oktober 1940.

DER OBER-ÄLTESTENRAT
DER JÜDISCHEN BEVÖLKERUNG
RADOM
DER VORSITZENDE
(–) JOSEF DIAMENT

OSTRZEŻENIE
do ludności żydowskiej.

Na skutek zarządzenia Arbeitsamtu w Radomiu podajemy do wiadomości, że począwszy od dnia dzisiejszego, wobec wszystkich, którzy nie stawią się do pracy lub rejestracji na wezwanie ARBEITSAMTU, stosowane będą najcięższe kary więzienne albo obozu koncentracyjnego.

Wobec tego wzywamy wszystkich zobowiązanych do stawienia się, aby BEZWARUNKOWO w ściśle oznaczonych terminach czynili zadość wezwaniu Arbeitsamtu.

Radom, dnia 18 października 1940 r.

In addition to acquisitions abroad, an important source of exhibits was the Holocaust-related memorabilia given to the Museum by survivors living in the United States. Many survivors came to regard the Museum as the appropriate repository for objects that linked them to this terrible period in their lives.

The actual availability of objects constituted one of the important considerations the team had to take into account when working on the exhibition segments. The boxcar, for instance, affected the circulation path, since visitors were to walk through it, and its height affected the building because in order to accommodate it, the floor had to be lowered. Another example is that the availability of the Auschwitz barracks made it possible to create a large environment within which camp-related artifacts could be displayed.

The extensive hunt for objects brought with it not only a multitude of potential exhibits but also many curious episodes that offered respite from the painful atmosphere that enveloped the team in its daily work on the Holocaust story.

A misunderstanding caused the Polish Commission for the Investigation of War Crimes to have the railway car painted with fresh, glowing red paint before it was sent as a present to Washington. It took several months and about $50,000 to have an expert conservator return it to its authentic condition by scraping off the new paint and revealing the underlying layer of its original color, so that the car eventually looked as it had during the war years.

When a staff member tried to obtain from a German anthropological institute a set of instruments used in the Nazi period for the measuring of "race characteristics"—eye color, hair color, width of nose—the elderly director of the anthropological institute, for reasons of his own, declined to hand over the instruments. One of his younger assistants, however, who apparently identified more with the intentions of the Museum than with those of her superior, eventually brought the instruments to the staff member. She probably succeeded in convincing her director that it would be wise to give the instruments to the Museum. They are now displayed in the Permanent Exhibition—each next to a photograph depicting their actual use in Nazi times.

Another memorable episode was the way the Museum got hold of the guest book from the Royal Hotel in Evian. In 1938 an international conference on refugees took place in that luxury hotel and researchers assumed that the hotel's guest book would carry the list of the conference participants. The Museum Director went to Evian, found the hotel, and asked the manager whether he knew about the important, historic conference that had made his hotel world famous. The manager admitted that he had never heard about it, and it took the hotel staff two days to find the 1938 guest book in one of their many storage rooms. It indeed contained the names of all conference participants, calligraphically listed, country by country. When asked to donate the book to the Museum, the manager refused: "Such an important historic document—how could we possibly give it away . . ." With the help of the French Ambassador to the United States, the hotel

Guest register from the Royal Hotel in Evian, France, with names of delegates to historic 1938 conference on refugees.

was eventually persuaded to yield the guest book, which is now displayed in the segment devoted to the Evian Conference.

The worldwide search for Holocaust-related artifacts was accompanied by a multitude of such episodes. Emotional meetings with survivors who came to the Museum to deposit cherished personal objects from their days in the ghetto, in the concentration camp, or in a hiding place, added deeply affecting moments to the hunt for potential exhibits. Each of these ordinary objects of everyday life had a story to tell that gave a glimpse into the most terrible time in the life of the survivor. Such meetings made the museum staff realize time and again that the chapter of history they were going to present in the exhibition is composed of countless individual emotional stories.

Above: Kitchen utensils confiscated from victims at Auschwitz.

Below: Violin used by inmate of Plaszow concentration camp to entertain Nazi officials at private parties.

Parallel to the search for artifacts, the planning team conducted an equally extensive search for photographs and film footage. In the United States, in Israel, and all over Europe, countless photo and film archives and numerous private collections were visited by team members who tried to solicit donations and negotiate purchases.

The search for photos and film footage yielded unexpected results. It provided the Museum with a wealth of material that enabled it to compose the visual story of the Holocaust. In the process, the Museum's photo archive was created. Today it holds many images never before exposed to the public eye. Most gratifying, however, was the successful search for film footage. Precious documentary film material was unearthed in German archives, including film fragments shot by Nazi soldiers who found pleasure in filming the atrocities they or their comrades perpetrated. Some of the most valuable material was detected and acquired by an outside production team commissioned to produce the film on the Nazis' rise to power and several short historical monitor programs for the Permanent Exhibition. The contractors found exquisite color film footage depicting Nazi parades, ceremonies, and festivities from the day of the takeover of power in 1933 to the end of the decade.

Four years of searching for exhibition material in many countries created a vast network of institutions and individuals who became aware of the Museum and linked to it in one way or another. The Museum became known worldwide long before it opened to the public. The search entailed international interaction between the Museum and a multitude of personalities and institutions.

AUDIOVISUAL PROGRAMS

During the stage of macro-design the team had to consider rules that would govern the use of sound and visual elements in the framework of audiovisual programs. From the outset it was clear that sound would not be the leading thread of the exhibition. Exhibitions are there to be seen, not to be told and listened to. The use of sound as the major carrier of the narrative also fragmentizes the exhibition visit: the cognitive absorption of content communicated by sound necessitates a level of concentration that cannot be reached in the course of a continuous walk through the exhibition galleries, with all the visual stimuli and the inevitable noise generated by other visitors. Moreover, exhibitions that rely on sound as the leading thread are forced to divide the walk-through into discrete story chapters, and the visitor who wants to follow the narrative cannot proceed to the next chapter before having heard all that is being said in the preceding one. Thus narrative-carrying sound organizes the visiting public into discrete groups and no visitor can see the exhibition at his or her own pace. In order to listen, visitors would have to sit down and the exhibition as a whole would, in the best case, become a sequence of sit-down theaters. The planning team actively wanted to avoid this.

The team understood, on the other hand, that sound can enrich an exhibition considerably when it is used as an atmospheric rather than a narrative component. That does not mean that it cannot carry speech; speaking voices, too, can contribute to the creation of atmosphere. However, such speech was not to be a necessary part of the story line. The planners would leave it up to individual visitors to decide whether or not they wanted to listen to the content of the speech or regard the voices as atmospheric background sound.

In line with these considerations, the first part of the Museum's Permanent Exhibition contains audiovisual programs not only with the music of Nazi marches but also with speeches of Nazi leaders like Hitler, Goebbels, and Streicher. Visitors who choose not to listen to the speeches can still absorb impressions about their quality and flavor, and about the image of the speakers. They certainly can still understand the flow of the narrative in its entirety. A sound program on life in Auschwitz later in the exhibition, composed of fragments of inmate testimonies, was given separate, closed space with seating facilities, across the aisle from the Auschwitz barracks.

Advanced audiovisual display technology is an important element in the macro-design of the exhibition. In addition to three short films and numerous interactive display facilities, the exhibition includes fifty-nine monitors with audiovisual programs integrated in the visitor's walk-through.

Why so many audiovisual programs? Audiovisual programs add a dynamic element to the visitor's experience during the walk-through. They insert motion into the static display of artifacts and photographic or textual panels, and thus strengthen the grip of the narrative on the visitor. Moving images let people identify more readily with what they see than do still photographs. Furthermore, monitor programs make it possible to present many images in relatively little wall space. Photographs are most effective in an exhibition when they are presented in large size. Consequently still photography consumes a great deal of wall space and severely limits the number of images that can be presented. Combining still photography with monitor programs greatly enhances not only the quality of the presentation but also the quantity of the presented visual material.

At the same time, the planning team was also aware that audiovisual monitor programs cannot be based on sequential plots that become meaningful only when seen from the beginning to the end. Visitors are liable to come upon the monitor when it is in the middle of the program. If the program's meaning hinges on sequence, visitors have to wait, more often than not, until the beginning of the next "performance." Programs had to be composed of randomly arranged images, so that visitors would be free to look at the program as little or as long as they desired. Thus audiovisual programs, similar to sound elements, could become important content carriers and greatly enrich the visitor's experience, but they themselves could not be given a narrative infrastructure.

Two very short plot-driven films were included in the Permanent Exhibition ("Nazi Rise to Power" and "Antisemitism") and are presented in enclosed mini-theaters. Both are complementary to the basic narrative; they are optional rather than necessary ingredients. On the other hand, there is a relatively long film at the end of the walk-through ("Testimony") that certainly is essential to the narrative. Its structure is a random arrangement of fragmentary eyewitness testimonies. Whenever visitors reach this point in the walk-through, they can sit down and view testimony fragments as long as they want, without having to wait for the beginning of the film. The film has no beginning and no end.

The younger generation is accustomed to the assimilation of knowledge through the use of audiovisual and interactive computerized devices. The United States Holocaust Memorial Museum speaks this language of the young, thus enhancing its ability to open the minds and hearts of the young to the history it presents.

Nazi propaganda minister Josef Goebbels addressing crowds in Berlin on anti-Jewish boycott day, April 1, 1933.

Facing page: Esther Terner Raab, survivor of Sobibor, from a section of the Permanent Exhibition testimony film.

The use of audiovisual devices, however, also has its dangers. Overwhelming visual predominance of high-tech elements can easily distract from content and draw attention to technological achievement. It can introduce a confusing, theme-park-like feel, giving a serious exhibition the trappings of an entertainment-oriented installation. Furthermore, in a Holocaust-related exhibition, the massive use of technical display devices would feel anachronistic and alienating. Even if each monitor made a meaningful contribution to the narrative, negative impressions could arise unless appropriate design aesthetics were employed. The monitors and projection screens had to be so well integrated into the design of the display that they did not dominate the overall picture. To prevent the feeling of technological glitz, or of incompatibility of technology and subject matter, the design of the Permanent Exhibition observed aesthetic austerity in placing its audiovisual equipment. The planners succeeded in avoiding the pitfalls of over-conspicuous technology, although the Museum does offer the visitor a large number of films, audiovisual programs, and interactive computer-based facilities.

THE CONTENT COMMITTEE

After the phase of macro-design was substantially completed, the designer, Ralph Appelbaum, built a 1:12 scale model of the planned exhibition. The exhibition model, along with model elements of the building and a demonstration unit of the Wexner Learning Center (the computerized interactive learning facility of the Museum) was installed in a large display room at 2000 L Street NW, a building that housed the Museum offices before the present administration offices were completed. For about three years the planning team used the models to explain what the exhibition was going to look like. Hundreds of people—Museum Council members, public personalities, prospective donors, journalists, museum professionals,

and others—were given the "model tour" in the planning stage of the Museum. Thus the model helped in the preparation of public opinion and in the creation of a large constituency of devotees long before the Museum opened to the public.

The model also played an important role in the exhibition planning approval process. The United States Holocaust Memorial Council's Museum Development Committee, which supervised the construction of the building and the creation of the Permanent Exhibition, appointed a Content Committee under the chairmanship of Council member Benjamin Meed. This was the watchdog committee whose task was to scrutinize and approve the content of the exhibition as proposed by the planning team. The Content Committee was composed of Jews and non-Jews. It counted among its members, in addition to the top leadership of the Council, eminent Holocaust scholars and several survivors. Having approved the proposed story line, the Committee judged the design proposals on the basis of the scale model.

Facing page: Hair shorn from the heads of female inmates of Auschwitz as displayed at the Auschwitz site museum.

Above: Hair, bagged and numbered for shipment to Germany

Both inside and outside the framework of the Content Committee's deliberations, many Holocaust scholars played an important role in providing the planning team with historical guidance and in constantly vetting the exhibition for historical reliability. Two of them became closely involved in the planning process in all its stages: Professor Raul Hilberg from the University of Vermont, the author of the famous work *The Destruction of the European Jews,* and Professor Israel Gutman of Hebrew University Jerusalem, the Director of the Holocaust Research Center of Yad Vashem, the Holocaust Martyrs' and Heroes' Memorial in Jerusalem.

The planning team always succeeded in obtaining the imprimatur of the Content Committee by consensus of all its members. Serious political sensitivities and tensions were inherent in the planning process, and the planners needed circumspect navigation to avoid shipwreck of the project. Only in one case was a controversy initially resolved by vote and majority decision. The planning team proposed to include the display of hair of female victims in the exhibition. A large display of such hair is on exhibit in the site museum of the Auschwitz death camp. The majority of the Committee approved the proposal, but two survivors from among the committee members appealed to the Museum Director, requesting reconsideration of the decision. They pointed out that hair was part of the human body, and out of respect for the visitors it should not be displayed as an exhibit. One of them said ". . . it may be my mother's or my sister's hair which you are going to exhibit." Since this was the only approval that was not obtained by consensus, the Director agreed to abandon the proposal, and the Committee voted at its next meeting unanimously for reversal of their decision. As a result, instead of real hair, the Museum displays a large photograph of the hair shown in the Auschwitz site museum.

Having approved the basic macro-design, the Committee continued to monitor design changes that arose in the course of the planning process.

While macro-design determines the character and sequence of the exhibition segments, micro-design focuses on the content of each segment down to the last detail. The main elements of micro-design were visuals (photographs, film footage, and sometimes maps), artifacts, and text.

Once the Museum entered the phase of micro-design, various departments became directly or indirectly involved in the design process, and various auxiliary units came into existence. The Collection Department supplied the artifacts; a small photo-research unit provided the still photographs, drawing material from the Photo Archive; and other units developed the maps and the audiovisual displays.

As mentioned before, works of art were not included in the Permanent Exhibition to preserve its documentary integrity and its validity as historical evidence and to avoid any impression of emotional manipulation. Only two exceptions were made to this rule: in the segment on West European internment camps, three small inmates' drawings, depicting camps in France, were included as substitutes for documentary photographs. And on the wall devoted to the fate of children in the Holocaust, a selection of children's drawings from the Terezin ghetto is displayed. These drawings, too, were considered as exhibits of documentary validity.

Visual Components

The narrative history museum is essentially an attempt at visual historiography. When dealing with modern times, photographs are the primary carriers of its narrative. However, as compared with written text, photographs are relatively primitive conveyors of historical content because they cannot express all the nuances which the written word can conjure. Up to a point, the exhibition can overcome shortcomings of visual expression through carefully researched captions.

Each of the many hundreds of photographs that found their place on the walls of the Permanent Exhibition were chosen in meetings of the planning team with the participation of the designer, Ralph Appelbaum. The team not only chose the photographs for their visual content but also developed guidelines about positioning them within their respective display segments. Although some team members frequently favored inclusion of vintage snapshots in their original small size, it was agreed, on the whole, that the exhibition needed large visuals, even if this meant displaying fewer photographs on walls and panels. Usually it was possible to include additional photographs in monitor programs.

The photo-research unit not only dug out the needed visuals from the huge piles offered by the Photo Archive but also researched the provenance and documentary reliability of each of them. In several cases the validation of photographs required veritable detective work. When assembling the material for an audiovisual program on the rescue of the Danish Jews, for example, the two staff members of the unit had to determine which of the photographs were historically genuine and which originated in a docudrama film depicting the rescue operation. Those staged for the film were naturally disqualified from inclusion in the exhibition. In another instance, only one labeled photograph was originally available for a monitor program on the infamous massacre in Babi Yar, near Kiev. The research unit, however, succeeded in identifying several unlabeled photographs of the Babi Yar ravine by discovering similarities in landscape with the one photograph that was clearly identified. This made it possible to install a Babi Yar monitor.

Some of the monitor programs were created by a small in-house production unit and the rest were made by professional production companies. The abundance of unique historic film footage that was made available by extensive research lent the programs a high degree of historical credibility. Members of the planning team actively participated in working with the outside producers. They made sure that the programs abided by the two overriding principles that guided the whole design process: absolute historical reliability and maximum clarity of communication. They also composed the captions for all programs. On the eve of the opening of the Museum, team members were still working in a film studio on the captioning of the last program.

Much work went into the preparation of maps and the supervision of their production. Maps constitute an important ingredient in any historical exhibition because they offer the visitor the geographical coordinates for the historical events depicted. Here, too, staff members who were charged specifically with the task of preparing the maps worked with an outsider, a cartographer, who provided the required professional service.

Artifacts

Authentic three-dimensional artifacts provide the strongest historical evidence, stronger even that documentary photographs. They constitute a direct link to the events, which are embedded in them, as it were. Having been there, they have become silent witnesses.

The artifacts were collected by the team or donated by survivors and liberators and were placed in the care of the Museum's Collections Department, which maintained two large storage facilities not far from Baltimore. A conservator was hired to organize the conservation work and later to supervise the proper maintenance of the artifacts once they were installed in the Museum building.

Throughout the micro-design process, the Exhibition Department searched its collection for artifacts that related in content to the various thematic segments of the exhibition. In special staging sessions, they laid the objects out on tables for the planning team to inspect and choose. These sessions were usually attended by many people—the extended planning team and most of the Collections Department's staff, together with other staff members who came to the storage facility to form sensory links with what many thought of as the "real material" of the exhibition. The discussions that evolved around the choice of objects frequently determined, to a far-reaching extent, the content and layout of the respective segments.

There was, for instance, a staging session devoted to material relating to the famous voyage of the *St. Louis*, the German steamer that in 1939 carried more than 900 Jewish refugees to safety in Havana, but had to take them back to Europe because they were refused landing rights in both Cuba and the United States. This was a much-mentioned event that has become metaphoric for the plight of the Jewish refugees from Nazi Germany and for the restrictive immigration policy of the United States. In view of the abundance of related artifacts, the exhibit presented the story of the *St. Louis* not only, as originally intended, through a sequence of large documentary photographs accompanied by an audiovisual program of stills and film footage, but also through a sequence of more than twenty artifacts that, with appropriate explanatory captions, would also convey the whole story. Among the available artifacts were the passenger list, snapshots of happy passengers taken on the way to Havana, optimistic cables sent to relatives, and then, when the crisis began, announcements by the captain and the exchange of cables between the passengers' committee and the "Joint." The Joint (short for Joint Jewish Distribution Committee) was the American Jewish organization that tried to obtain entrance visas for the refugees and eventually succeeded in preventing their return to Germany by getting permission to divide them among England, Holland, Belgium, and France. Thus, as a result of the staging session, the segment became a story told in two layers: one layer of visuals and one of artifacts.

Detail from the display on Nazi "race science."

In another case, the staging of textbooks on "race science"—didactic slides used in anthropological institutes, popular posters, and measuring instruments related to this Nazi pseudoscience—made it possible to discuss and determine on the spot the positioning of the objects and the layout of the race segment in its entirely. Many such staging sessions led directly to design decisions about whole thematic segments.

After the staging sessions, the chosen objects usually underwent appropriate conservation work before being installed in the exhibition. The amount of conservation work that had to be carried out was enormous. Four thousand victims' shoes from the death camp of Majdanek that were to fill one of the tower rooms had to be cleaned one by one. Each of the tens of striped uniforms once worn by inmates of concentration camps and now destined to become a display mounted in a three-floor deep shaft and visible both at the beginning of the walk-through and towards its end had to be individually stabilized to prevent further disintegration. Conservation work also had to be performed on many of the posters carrying official announcements from wartime Poland and the Ukraine that found their place in the ghetto section of the Permanent Exhibition.

Aware of the fact that large exhibits are visually much more impressive and effective than small ones, the planning team tried to obtain as many large objects as possible for inclusion in the exhibition. The Polish boxcar, the Auschwitz barracks, and the Danish fisher boat have already been mentioned. But there were many more. Tree stems from the Rudniki forest in Soviet Lithuania, in which Jewish partisan units operated during the war, were brought to Washington with the help of a forester and a Finnish transportation company; the Polish boxcar was placed on rails removed from the railway station of the Treblinka death camp; the gate to the Jewish cemetery of Tarnow, through which thousands of Jews were led to their execution, was placed in the ghetto section next to the entrance door to the Jewish hospital in Lodz, which also was the site of a terrible massacre; and a Gypsy wagon was brought from Czechoslovakia. There are many other examples.

In some cases the almost obsessive quest for large artifacts led to the acquisition of objects that had only dubious value for the exhibition, as in the case of the burned-out fragment of a German missile produced by slave laborers in the concentration cap of Dara-Mittelbau. The missile fragment became the subject of heated discussions among the members of the planning team, but eventually it was decided that it should not be included in the exhibition because, as a nondescript fragment of burned metal, it did not carry any illustration value.

On the other hand, there was widespread sentiment among team members for small personal Holocaust memorabilia. This was perhaps understandable from the human point of view, since many of the small objects represented very touching stories. The decision-making process that eventually led to the clear and convincing visual narrative of the Permanent Exhibition also had to relate to the emotional attitudes of staff. In a few cases, the outcome of the argument of emotion versus method was resolved by a compromise, as in the case of the children's wall on the lower exhibition floor, which includes several small showcases with personal memorabilia.

Textual Components

Just as people go to museums and exhibitions not to listen but to see, they do not go there to read. Those who want to read about the Holocaust seek out books or go to archives. This is why exhibitions should be very sparing in the display of text.

Textual display elements fall into two categories: textual exhibits, i.e. authentic textual documents displayed in the course of the visually presented narrative; and explanatory textual elements, i.e. text panels, labels, and captions authored by Museum staff or consultants to enrich the visual narrative and to facilitate its being fully understood by the visitor.

There is a natural inclination to include in historical exhibitions important documents, letters, and other textual exhibits pertaining to the subject matter. It is, however, a fact that most visitors do not read this kind of material, important as it may be. As a rule, in the course of a museum walk-through, visitors cannot summon the patience, nor the power of concentration, needed to read textual documents, which are usually written in small letters. This is why the Permanent Exhibition of the Museum includes very few written or typed documents, and even those few are probably read only by a small number of people.

Visitors usually do, however, read wall inscriptions, provided they are relatively short and presented in large type. Such wall inscriptions, although textual in form, can become as attractive to the visitor as visuals. They can indeed be considered a special category of visual exhibits. Thus a considerable number of significant wall inscriptions have been included in the Permanent Exhibition, such as quotes from speeches by Hitler and quotes from books by eminent survivor authors like Primo Levi and Elie Wiesel. The last wall inscription in the walk-through is a famous quote attributed to the anti-Nazi German Protestant pastor Martin Niemoeller: "First they came for the socialists, and I did not speak out—because I was not a socialist. Then they came for the trade unionists, and I did not speak out—because I was not a trade unionist. Then they came for the Jews, and I did not speak out—because I was not a Jew. Then they came for me—and there was no one left to speak for me." It was hard to find a better way to expose the guilt of the bystanders.

But while textual exhibits other than wall inscriptions should be kept to a bare minimum, textual elements of explanatory character fulfill vital functions in the narrative museum. Only words can provide the visitor with information on the historical background of the visuals and on the context in which they are displayed. When skillfully composed, explanatory panels provide the sequential links between the thematic segments.

Admittedly, there are always some who read many of the textual panels. Surely most visitors read the ones of particular interest to them. But whether written with the devoted or occasional reader in mind, explanatory text cannot be discursive, let alone long-winded. The style has to acknowledge that its reader is standing in the middle of a walk-through rather than at leisure. Most important, the text must be easily comprehensible, short, and terse, more like "speech bullets" than customary descriptive prose.

In the particular case of the United States Holocaust Memorial Museum, it was also important that the text be stylistically compatible with the general spirit of the exhibition whose power lies very much in understatement. It took much editorial work to eliminate from the text every bit of hyperbole. Keeping the language concise and factual allowed the historic events to speak for themselves without being dramatized by emotional verbal comment.

But although it seems that in the Holocaust Museum more explanatory text is being read than in most museums, even here the rule applies that visitors, on the whole, are not inclined to read while walking through an exhibition. Most of them seem to read every word during the very first part of their walk-through, and then limit themselves mainly to looking at the exhibits. Large-type panel titles define the theme of the segment to which the explanatory text relates and give the visitors the basic information they need to properly understand the flow of the narrative. The sequence of panel titles represents the infrastructure of the narrative display, just as the sequence of chapter titles usually represents the infrastructure of a book. Thus panel titles also help visitors better understand and internalize the structure of the exhibition. It is the job of the labels, in contrast, to properly identify the exhibits for the visitors.

Exhibitions are instruments of communication and exhibition design is a discipline of aesthetics. Ideally, exhibition design would combine a high level of aesthetics with clear communication. But too often designers focus on aesthetics, often to the detriment of communication. So the client has to represent the goal of clear communication in the client-designer relationship, just as the client has to be the guardian of functionality in the relationship with an architect. When there is a clash between aesthetics and communication, it is up to the museum to make sure that communication prevails. Clarity in presenting information is of much greater importance in a narrative exhibition than in a collection-based one because it relies on an elaborate system of explanatory text panels, labels, and captions for meaning. In the case of the United States Holocaust Memorial Museum, the planning team was not insistent enough in the pursuit of clear communication. As a result, even after the opening of the Museum, retrofit work aimed at improving the communication effectiveness of some of the text elements continued for a long time: exhibit titles in large type had to be added, text panels had to be relocated, and other such changes had to be made.

From Design to Installation

Whereas the sequence of thematic exhibition segments was defined in the macro-design phase, the choice of specific exhibit elements for each segment was the planning team's concern in the micro-design phase.

Once the planning team had chosen individual exhibits to be included in a segment, the designer, Ralph Appelbaum, was asked to propose a design frame to combine these exhibits into a discrete display unit. He submitted proposals for the design of segments to the team in the form of sketches or mock-ups. The planning team, which considered itself responsible for both historical content and aesthetic form, then scrutinized each proposal. Frequently the designer, who was a de facto team member, made changes in the original proposal in view of the team's critical observations. The final approval of segment design—a process that stretched out over a long period of time—concluded the phase of micro-design. Only the development of the audiovisual programs was left; it was being carried out in a parallel working process under the supervision of the same team.

The planning team's work in the micro-design phase entailed many heated discussions and although in principle it was desirable to let all team members participate democratically in the creative effort, decision-making in large committee proved to be difficult. The main reason was that decisions frequently called for aesthetic—and therefore necessarily subjective—judgment. Thus, while the interdisciplinary composition of the large team brought important intellectual and professional input from many domains, the final decision remained essentially in the hands of the core team, the team's small leading group. Only two members of the team had previous experience in museum planning—the Museum Director and the designer.

Once the planning team agreed on the proposed display design, Ralph Appelbaum's office in New York sent approved drawings to Maltbie Associates, an exhibition fabricator in New Jersey, which produced all components of the exhibition except the objects, the photographs, and the audiovisual components. One of the co-owners of Maltbie Associates, Gerhard Vogel, a Jewish refugee from Nazi Germany who survived the Holocaust in Shanghai, personally supervised his company's work for the Museum. He was devoted to the Museum far beyond the call of business. So was Stephen Weitz of St. Louis, Missouri, who fabricated pro bono the thousands of photographic reproductions that were included in the exhibition.

Fabrication was followed by exhibition installation, accomplished in an orchestrated joint effort of the planning team, the Museum's Collections Department, the fabricator's team, the designer's team, and a special team of exhibit-mounting experts. Installation lasted several months and led to many minor changes in the design of individual segments. The effort at improving the quality of the exhibition by appropriate changes in design details continued long after the opening of the Museum.

THE VISITOR AND THE VICTIM

Throughout the planning process, staff had to wrestle with the question of how to project the human face of the victim. To facilitate the emotional identification process, it was essential that visitors perceive the victims as human individuals rather than as a mass of dehumanized, emaciated creatures or unclothed corpses, the way they appear in most photographs and films portraying concentration camps in the days of liberation. Statistics are emotionally quite meaningless: as a French general put it during the First World War: "One person killed is a tragedy—ten thousand killed is statistics." It was one of the main objectives of the planning team to show the visitor not just the horror of the mass killing but also the human nature, the human faces of those who

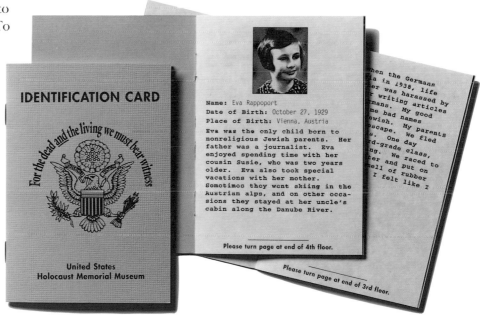

I.D. cards with stories of Holocaust victims and survivors, distributed at the entrance of the Permanent Exhibition.

were killed. Certain design strategies were adopted to serve this purpose of helping visitors balance in their minds the overwhelming impression of the numbers and the identification with the individual victim.

In various exhibits the victims are shown as they looked and lived before the war, before they were victimized. The segment "Life before the Holocaust," which consists of five monitor programs, confronts visitors with photographs from Jewish life in the various regions of Europe and in North Africa. Another segment, "On the Eve of Destruction," portrays traditional orthodox Jewry in prewar Eastern Europe as observed by the well-known photographer Roman Vishniac. Admittedly, it is not in the power of these two relatively small segments to drive home the important point that the Holocaust destroyed not only one-third of the Jewish population, but also the rich Yiddish culture of Eastern European Jewry. Yiddish, which was before the war the language of millions of Jews is now hardly spoken anymore anywhere. There was great Yiddish literature, Yiddish poetry, Yiddish theater, and a Yiddish press—all this no longer exists. Together with Yiddish culture, the Nazis also destroyed the culture based on Ladino, the language of Sephardic Jews in South Eastern Europe—Yugoslavia, Greece, and Bulgaria. But though perhaps deplorably inadequate in presenting the tragedy of the destruction of Jewish culture in Europe, these segments do serve the purpose of portraying the human face of the living Jew.

The most important exhibition segment aimed at humanizing the image of the victim is the three-floor-high "Tower of Faces," whose walls are covered by about one thousand prewar photographs of Jewish inhabitants from the Lithuanian town of Eiszyszki, whose whole Jewish population—3,500 hundred men, women, and children—were slaughtered by the Germans in two days. Only 29 escaped. The photographs were collected over many years by Professor Yaffa Eliach of Brooklyn College, one of the few survivors of the Eiszyszki massacre. The "Tower of Faces" is one of the most impressive exhibits of the Museum.

To personalize the concept of victims, the visitor, on entering the Permanent Exhibition, receives an "ID card" of a person who was caught up in the Holocaust. The card carries a photograph of the person and tells how he or she perished or survived. The visitor then goes through the exhibition of the Holocaust with a companion, as it were. As told by the Museum, the story reveals both the breakdown of civilization and the plight of the human being.

The most important elements that personalize the Holocaust are the "oral histories," the audio or video testimonies of survivors. In a sound program, inmates tell visitors about their experience in the Auschwitz death camp, and at the end of the walk-through visitors are invited to take a seat in an amphitheater and see a program of survivors discussing episodes of rescue and resistance. This program, which carries the title "Testimony," is considered by many as the strongest single exhibit in the whole exhibition.

The intention to counteract a dehumanized image of the victim also thoroughly affected the design style of the exhibition. The planning team strived to minimize graphic depictions of Holocaust horrors. They were included only as much as was deemed to be absolutely necessary for reasons of documentation, so as not to sanitize the Holocaust. Even so, almost all photographs of naked corpses found by the Allied armies or of the gruesome medical experiments carried out by Nazi doctors in the concentration camps are shown behind protection walls, so visitors are aware that they are about to be confronted with emotionally difficult exhibits and can decide whether they want to be exposed to them.

AMERICANS ENCOUNTER THE CAMPS

OHRDRUF
CONCENTRATION
CAMP

THE HOLOCAUST

The things I saw beggar description. . . .The visual evidence and the verbal testimony of starvation, cruelty and bestiality were. . . .overpowering. . . .I made the visit deliberately in order to be in position to give firsthand evidence of these things if ever, in the future, there develops a tendency to charge these allegations merely to "propaganda."

General Dwight D. Eisenhower, April 15, 1945

In a letter to Chief of Staff George Marshall, General Eisenhower described the horrors he witnessed at Ohrdruf, a Nazi slave-labor camp in Germany. Museum visitors encounter this prophetic quotation at the beginning of the Permanent Exhibition.

BUCHENWALD
CONCENTRATION
CAMP

After liberation, a U.S. Army photographer took this picture of a starved
concentration camp inmate. Buchenwald, Germany, 1945. National
Archives, Washington, D.C.

A starved prisoner of Buchenwald has received
a meal from Allied liberators.

A three-story shaft within the Permanent
Exhibition displays uniforms worn by inmates
of concentration camps.

Exhibits along this introductory corridor describe
the beginnings of Nazi rule in Germany.

Hitler's rise to power in 1933 marked the end of parliamentary government in Germany. Here, a member of the SS accompanies a German policeman on patrol. When the Nazi private army joined the civil police, political violence became governmentally sanctioned.

On April 1, 1933, the Nazis announced an official boycott of Jewish businesses throughout Germany. The boycott represented a major step in a national campaign against the German Jewish community. Those who dared to defy the boycott encountered storm troopers in uniforms such as this.

Overleaf: Photographs, artifacts and film clips describe Nazi use of propaganda and terror to propound their political and racist ideologies.

Political violence became official when members of the SA and the SS were drafted as auxiliary police. Here, an SS man accompanies a policeman. Berlin, March 8, 1933. *Bundesarchiv Koblenz, Germany*

Michalski & Striemer
konfektionierte Weisswaren
Kinderhüte
FAHRSTUHL

...he, verteidigt Euch
...en die jüdifche
...uel propaganda,
fauft
...ei Deutfchen

...rmans defend
...lves against jew
...ity propaganda
...y at German shops!

Most Germans who tried to enter Jewish-owned shops on Ap...
encountered storm troopers in uniforms such as this. It was t...
worn by a "troop leader" in SA Group 5 of the Berlin-Brandenb...
The abbreviation "SA" stood for *Sturmabteilung*, or "attack de...

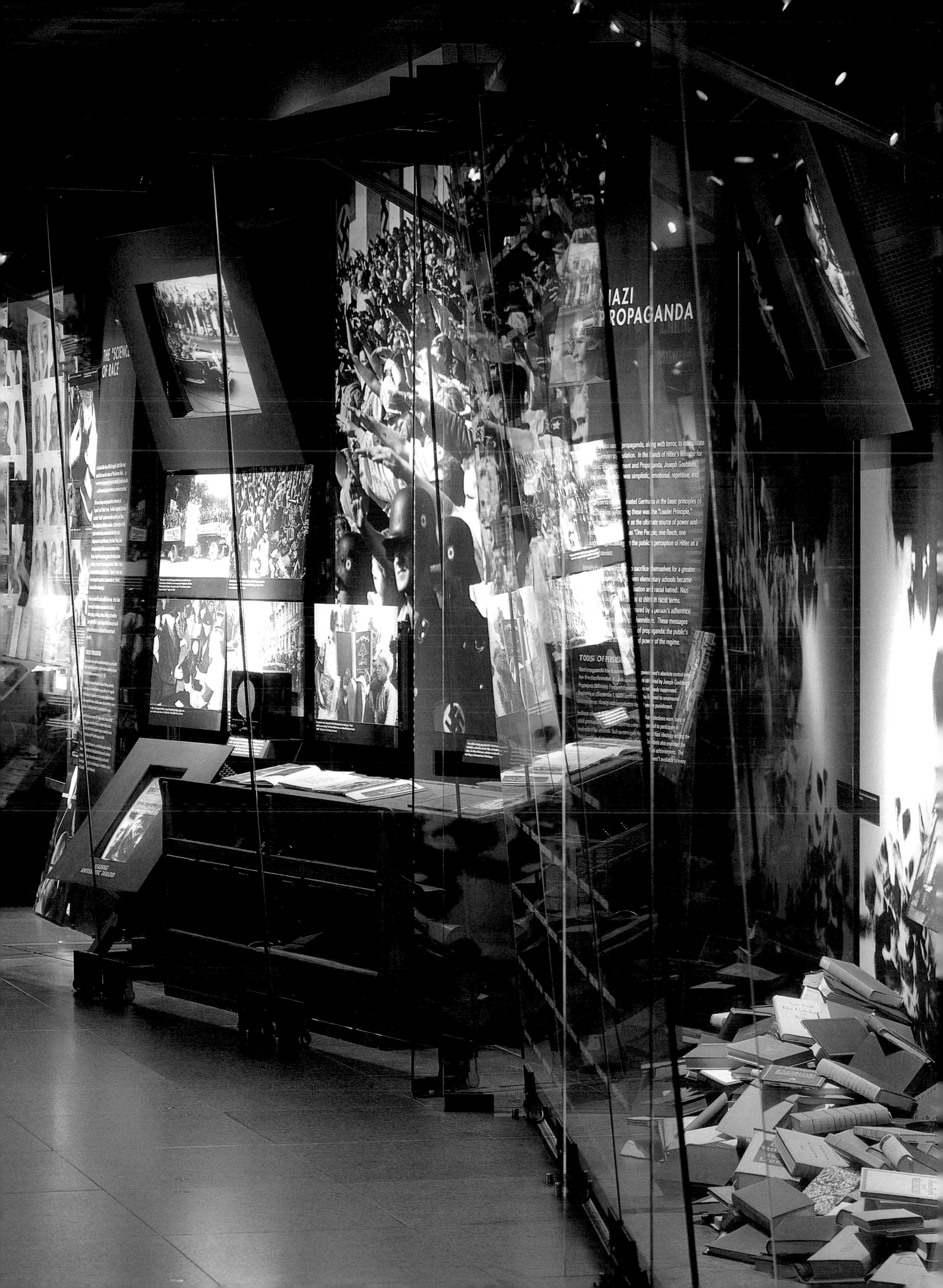
PROPAGANDA
OF RACE

Nazi party officials and student organizations raided libraries and bookstores across Germany burning books deemed "un-German." The books piled in front of these photographs represent a few of the thousands of titles banned by the Nazis, including works by American authors Helen Keller, Jack London, Sinclair Lewis, and Ernest Hemingway.

Through state-controlled news media, countless parades, speeches, ceremonies, and events, the Nazis influenced the German population. These children's books were intended to foster in young Germans a sense of nationalism, anti-semitism, and allegiance to Hitler.

These children's books were intended to indoctrinate young Germans in nationalism, antisemitism, love for Hitler, and obedience to his will. They include *The Poison Mushroom*, a collection of antisemitic stories; and *Read Along!*, an illustrated book of Nazi slogans.

German schools played a political ideology. These from German classrooms *Mahn- und Gedenkstätte* donated by the Akademi

...gy from an early age. These
...om, an antisemitic picture book.

Berlin, 1937. Abraham Pisarek Collection, Berlin

Eye-color selection guide on loan from Dr. Friedrich Rösing

Throughout Nazi Germany, racial specialists examined eye and hair color and measured facial dimensions in order to determine whether individuals were racially "Aryan" or "alien." A series of decrees and laws treated persons of "superior" and "inferior" race differently. Many Germans went to pains to prove their "Aryan" ancestry.

Germany, 1937. Bil...

Caliper for measuring nose wi...
Humangenetik...

Nazi theories of Aryan supremacy gave rise to a pseudo-science of racial studies. Instruments such as these (left) measured facial characteristics in order to distinguish members of "inferior" or alien races from "superior" Aryans. Beginning in January 1934, the quest for racial purity led to forced sterilization of those considered "abnormal."

Neger
(Herero)

Melanefier
(Salomo-Infeln)

Pygmäe
(Zentralafrika)

Oftifch
(Litauer)

Mittelländifch (Weftifch)
(Süddeutscher, Salzburger)

Dinarifch
(Albaner)

Wenn Juden lachen

Lesen Sie die neueste Ausgabe 11 des Stürmers

The Nazi tabloid *Der Stürmer* (The Attacker) propagated racial stereotypes of Jews. This poster advertising *Der Stürmer* stated that because Jews are "born criminals," they cannot laugh but can only twist their faces in "a devilish grin."

These charts reflected the official Nazi view that human races were as different as species. Nazi theoreticians identified the "Nordic," "Falian," and "Dinaric" races, among others, as races of Europe.

Hundreds of pseudoscientific works on "racial studies" (*Rassenkunde*) appeared under Nazi rule, including such titles as The Nordic Soul and Race and Character. One of the most prolific authors was Hans F. K. Günther, who also served on a council that advised the regime about "racial hygiene" policy.

Between 1933 and 1939, the Nazis reversed a century of equal opportunity for German Jews, enacting over 400 laws designed to define, segregate, and impoverish German Jews. Jews were forced to carry identification cards such as these, marked with the letter "J". Public areas, like the bench pictured here, were designated for Jews only.

Of the thirty-three nations invited to the Evian conference to discuss the growing refugee crisis in Europe, only the tiny Dominican Republic offered to receive substantial numbers of Jews. Despite mounting pressure, the U.S. maintained strict immigration quotas. This exhibit displays the guest book from the luxurious Hotel Royal in Evian, which contains the names of conference delegates.

ESSEN SYNAGOGUE — AFTER THE NOVEMBER POGROM

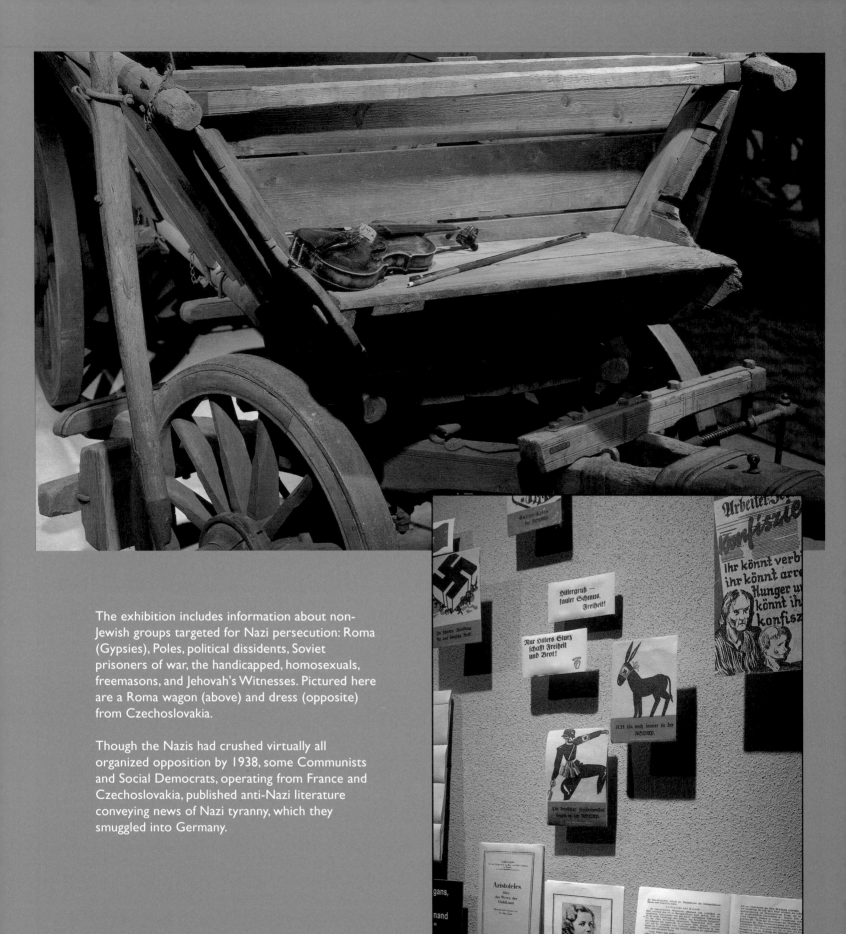

The exhibition includes information about non-Jewish groups targeted for Nazi persecution: Roma (Gypsies), Poles, political dissidents, Soviet prisoners of war, the handicapped, homosexuals, freemasons, and Jehovah's Witnesses. Pictured here are a Roma wagon (above) and dress (opposite) from Czechoslovakia.

Though the Nazis had crushed virtually all organized opposition by 1938, some Communists and Social Democrats, operating from France and Czechoslovakia, published anti-Nazi literature conveying news of Nazi tyranny, which they smuggled into Germany.

Nazis designated Gypsies (Roma) as "Asocials." After 1935, Roma were registered on "racial grounds" for arrest, sterilization and deportation.

This is a portrait of Antonia Steinbach, one of the 22,000 German Roma (Gypsies) defrauded by the Nazis in the 1930s and 1940s. She died at the Bergen-Belsen concentration camp in March 1945, shortly before liberation.

ROMA (GYPSIES)

Roma were subjected to official discrimination well before 1933. ("Roma" is the term preferred by "Gypsies" themselves.) After Hitler took power, long-held prejudices were fueled by Nazi racism, although no comprehensive anti-Roma law was ever passed.

Local initiatives against Roma preceded policy decisions from Berlin. The city of Frankfurt, for example, established an internment camp for Roma in 1935. The following year, it banned settlement of additional Roma within the city limits.

In 1938, the Reich Interior Ministry issued guidelines titled "On Combating the Gypsy Plague," which mandated the fingerprinting and photographing of Roma. Beginning in 1937, the Nazi regime used these records to imprison Roma in concentration camps. The measures were intended to counter the perceived threat that Roma posed to German "racial purity." One Nazi racial theorist further urged: "In the long term, the German people will be freed from this public nuisance only when [the Gypsies'] fertility is completely eliminated."

Photographs, film, and text describe German
society, nearly every aspect of which was subject to
Nazification under Hitler's rule. The Gestapo, the
secret state police, were vested with almost
unlimited authority to monitor the activities of all
citizens and to impose arrest without warrant.

German parliament was little more than a sounding ...ches. The dictator is visible on the left side of the ...ay 21, 1935. *Ullstein Bilderdienst, Berlin*

German men between the ages of 18 and 25 had to serve for one year in the paramilitary Reich Labor Service. Here, a Labor Service contingent marches in review at the 1937 Nazi party rally. Nuremberg, September 8, 1937. *AP/Wide World Photos, New York*

This banner once flew over Hitler's mountain retreat near Berchtesgaden, in Bavaria. In 1920, at Hitler's urging, the Nazi party adopted the swastika as its official symbol. A law passed on September 15, 1935—the same date as the Nuremberg Laws—declared the Nazi banner to be the national flag of Germany.

Louis shows the passenger cabins on the ship's

The *St. Louis* was under the command of Captain Gustav Schröder. Throughout the trip, Schröder treated his passengers with kindness and respect. This cap belonged to him.

Belgium took in 214 refugees, the Netherlands 181, Britain 287, and France 224. Hundreds of the refugees perished later in the Holocaust. Antwerp, Belgium, June 17, 1939. *Centre de Recherches et d'Études historiques de la Seconde Guerre Mondiale, Brussels, Belgium*

In 1939, a German steamer, the *St. Louis*, sought refuge in Havana for its 900 Jewish passengers. Although the passengers held Cuban visas, landing rights were abruptly canceled by the Cuban government when the ship attempted to dock. The *St. Louis* then sought refuge in Miami but was again turned away, this time by the United States, and was ultimately forced to return to Europe. Though the passengers found refuge in Belgium, England, France, and Holland, about half of them eventually ended up in Nazi death camps. The story of the *St. Louis* became a metaphor for the plight of Jewish refugees and continues to frame discussion of U.S. immigration policies today.

At great risk because of their politics and publications, European Jewish and non-Jewish writers, philosophers, artists, and intellectuals fled the continent. Cultural life in the United States and Great Britain benefited enormously from the contributions of such refugees as Albert Einstein, Sigmund Freud, Thomas Mann, Marc Chagall, Max Ernst, and others.

TO SAFETY

During the 1930s and 1940s, many of Europe's finest artists, writers, musicians, scholars, and scientists became refugees. Threatened because they were Jews or because their work was unacceptable to the Nazis, they sought safety in exile. Though many countries were reluctant to take in ordinary Jewish refugees, a few willingly accepted renowned Jewish artists and intellectuals.

In the United States, the Emergency Visitors' Visa Program was established to save "persons of exceptional merit" and "those of superior intellectual attainment." The Emergency Rescue Committee, a private organization, sent a young editor, Varian Fry, to Europe in 1940 to help emigrés escape the Nazis. Fry enabled nearly 2,000 people to flee.

The exiled playwright Bertolt Brecht reflected:

  I know, of course; it's simply luck
  That I've survived so many friends. But last night in a
  dream
  I heard those friends say of me: "Survival of the fittest,"
  And I hated myself.

AN EXODUS OF CULTURE

At risk because of their politics and publications, the German authors Thomas Mann and Heinrich Mann and the theologian Paul Tillich left Germany in 1933. The Jewish writer Lion Feuchtwanger emigrated to America. The novelist Arnold Zweig and Max Brod, the biographer of Franz Kafka, departed for Palestine. Albert Einstein left in 1933, settling in Princeton, New Jersey. Franz Werfel, the author of a novel about the Armenian genocide, *The 40 Days of Musa Dagh*, also emigrated to the United States.

As the territory of Nazi Germany expanded, the number of thinkers and writers seeking asylum grew. After the annexation of Austria in 1938, Sigmund Freud, the founder of psychoanalysis, left for England, as did the author Stefan Zweig. The exodus of European artists included Jean Arp, Max Beckmann, André Breton, Marc Chagall, Marcel Duchamp, Max Ernst, George Grosz, Jacques Lipchitz, André Masson.

European society and culture suffered from the loss of so many intellects and artists. Cultural life in the United States and Great Britain benefited enormously from the immigration of these and other luminaries.

Walter Hasenclever, Writer

EXILES

The physicist Albert Einstein was in California when Hitler came to power in January 1933. On his way back to Germany in March, Einstein decided instead not to return to the United States. Antwerp, Belgium, March 28, 1933. YIVO Institute for Jewish Research, New York

In June 1938, Sigmund Freud, the founder of psychoanalysis, emigrated with his daughter Anna from Vienna to London. This photograph shows them en their train enroute Paris. Paperfoto, Dresden, England

A desire for knowledge for its own sake, a love of justice that borders on fanaticism, and a striving for personal independence—these are the aspects of the Jewish people's tradition that allow me to regard my belonging to it as a gift of great fortune.

Those who today rage against the ideals of reason and individual freedom and who seek by means of brutal force to bring about a vapid state-slavery are justified in perceiving us as their implacable enemies. History has imposed on us a difficult struggle; but so long as we remain devoted servants of truth, justice, and freedom, we will not only persist as the oldest of living peoples, but will also continue as before to achieve, through productive labor, works that contribute to the ennoblement of humanity.

Albert Einstein (1879–1955),
Nobel laureate

The Nazis considered the Poles fit only to serve as slave laborers. In the spring of 1940, the German occupation government initiated a campaign to kill Polish priests, teachers, writers, artists, politicians, and suspected resistance members.

This tree stump (lower right) marked the site of a mass grave near the village of Palmiry where the Germans executed nearly 2,000 Poles in 1939 and 1940.

In the spring of 1940, the Nazi occupation authorities in Poland initiated a campaign to kill Polish priests, teachers, writers, artists, politicians, and suspected resistance members. The photograph was taken shortly before these SS men killed their blindfolded captives. Palmiry, 1940? *Main Commission for the Investigation of Nazi War Crimes in Poland, Warsaw*

This tree stump marked the site of a mass grave near the village of Palmiry, in Poland. German security police executed almost 2,000 Poles there in 1939 and 1940.

The physically and mentally disabled were the first victims of systematic Nazi murder under a program code-named "Operation T-4." This bed, blanket, and doctor's smock were taken from Sachsenberg clinic, a medical facility which was converted into an "Operation T-4" center where disabled children were killed by lethal injection.

Overleaf: At the conclusion of the fourth floor of the exhibition, Hitler is pictured here receiving a field briefing in western Germany. With him are the Nazi construction coordinator Fritz Todt; Nazi party secretary Martin Bormann; SS chief Heinrich Himmler; and military commander-in-chief General Wilhelm Keitel.

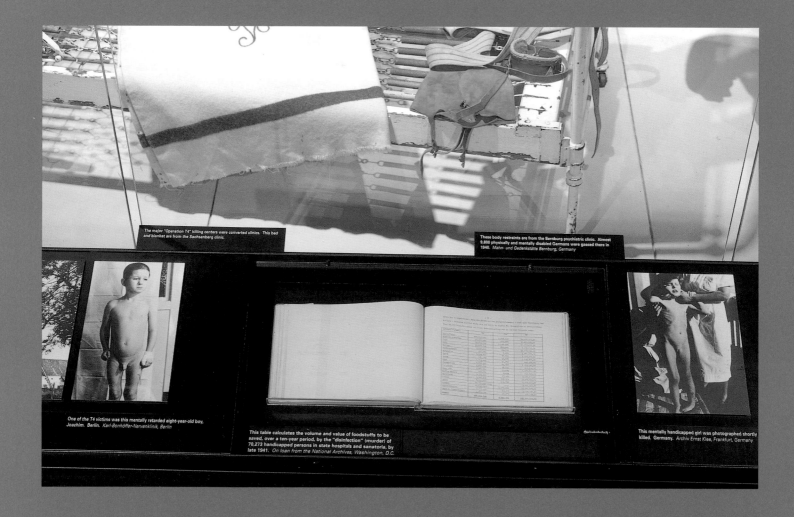

The major "Operation T4" killing centers were converted clinics. This bed and blanket are from the Sachsenberg clinic.

These body restraints are from the Bernburg psychiatric clinic. Almost 9,800 physically and mentally disabled Germans were gassed there in 1940. Mahn- und Gedenkstätte Bernburg, Germany

One of the T4 victims was this mentally retarded eight-year-old boy, Joachim. Berlin. Karl-Bonhöffer-Nervenklinik, Berlin

This table calculates the volume and value of foodstuffs to be saved, over a ten-year period, by the "disinfection" (murder) of 70,273 handicapped persons in state hospitals and sanatoria, by late 1941. On loan from the National Archives, Washington, D.C.

This mentally handicapped girl was photographed shortly killed. Germany. Archiv Ernst Klee, Frankfurt, Germany

I HAVE ISSUED THE COMMAND—AND I'LL HAVE ANYBODY WHO UTTERS BUT ONE WORD OF CRITICISM EXECUTED BY A FIRING SQUAD—THAT OUR WAR AIM DOES NOT CONSIST IN REACHING CERTAIN LINES, BUT IN THE PHYSICAL DESTRUCTION OF THE ENEMY. ACCORDINGLY, I HAVE PLACED MY DEATH-HEAD FORMATIONS IN READINESS—FOR THE PRESENT ONLY IN THE EAST—WITH ORDERS TO THEM TO SEND TO DEATH MERCILESSLY AND WITHOUT COMPASSION, MEN, WOMEN, AND CHILDREN OF POLISH DERIVATION AND LANGUAGE. ONLY THUS SHALL WE GAIN THE LIVING SPACE [LEBENSRAUM] WHICH WE NEED. WHO, AFTER ALL, SPEAKS TODAY OF THE ANNIHILATION OF THE ARMENIANS?

ADOLF HITLER, AUGUST 22, 1939, ACCORDING TO REPORTS RECEIVED BY THE ASSOCIATED PRESS BUREAU CHIEF IN BERLIN, LOUIS LOCHNER

Only guard yourself and guard your soul carefully, lest you forget the things your eyes saw, and lest these things depart your heart all the days of your life, and you shall make them known to your children, and to your children's children.

Deuteronomy 4:9

This three-story tower displays photographs from the Yaffa Eliach Shtetl Collection. Taken between 1890 and 1941 in Eishishok, a small town in what is now Lithuania, they describe a vibrant Jewish community which existed for 900 years. In 1941, an SS mobile killing squad entered the village and within two days massacred the Jewish population.

One of the many German Jewish children forced out of their homes, Anne Frank and her family fled to Amsterdam soon after Hitler's rise to power. In 1942, the Franks went into hiding. In 1944, a neighbor informed the Nazis of the Franks' whereabouts, and the family was sent first to Westerbork and then to Auschwitz. Anne and her sister, Margot, were subsequently deported to Bergen Belsen in 1944 where they died four weeks before British forces liberated the camp.

Overleaf: Throughout Eastern Europe, the Nazis segregated Jews in ghettos where overcrowding and squalor led to disease and starvation. Two photo murals depict life in the Warsaw ghetto (left) and the Lodz ghetto (right). In the latter, a "non-Jewish" street passed through the ghetto, and Jews were forced to use a wooden bridge, pictured here, to cross the prohibited thoroughfare. This bridge inspired the design of the wooden walkway visitors traverse through this part of the exhibition.

CONTAINER FROM
THE HIDDEN
WARSAW GHETTO
ARCHIVE

The Ringelblum milk can is perhaps the Museum's most important historic artifact. Under the leadership of Emmanuel Ringelblum, a university-trained historian, several dozen writers, teachers, rabbis, and historians compiled an archive documenting life in the Warsaw ghetto. When the destruction of the ghetto seemed imminent, they hid their diaries, documents, posters, and papers in milk cans and metal boxes, burying them beneath Warsaw streets. Ringelblum was shot by the Nazis in 1944; this can, one of those buried by Ringelblum and his colleagues, was discovered in 1950. Behind the Ringelblum milk can is a cast of the Warsaw ghetto wall, an 11-foot high barrier erected by the Nazis to confine Jewish inhabitants. This cast was made from the largest remaining segment of the wall.

The images on the large video monitors document the conditions of ghetto life.

In April 1940, the Nazis sealed the Lodz ghetto, trapping 164,000 Jews. Leon Jacobson, a Holocaust survivor, ghetto inmate, and shoemaker, fashioned this model of the Lodz ghetto out of leather. Shaped according to the outline of the ghetto walls, the model shows the locations of footbridges, ruined synagogues, factories and cemeteries; inside the model cover are official ghetto seals, ghetto currency, and a ration card.

MOBILE KILLING SQUADS

As German troops invaded Soviet territory in the summer of 1941, they were accompanied by specially trained mobile squads that had been assigned to kill all Jews, Communist party officials, and Roma (Gypsies) in the conquered areas. These units entered towns, cities, and villages shortly after their occupation by the German army.

The extermination operations followed a standard procedure. The unit's men rounded up the victims, drove them on foot or in trucks to a secluded site, made them remove their clothes, and shot them. Their corpses were buried in large pits, which the victims themselves had often been forced to dig.

Local Ukrainian, Latvian, Lithuanian, Estonian, and Belorussian collaborators and police volunteered their services to the killing squads and gave auxiliary support. In some places, the squads encouraged local pogroms. Waffen-SS (Armed SS) and German police units also took an active part in the mass murders. The German army often cooperated as well.

More than 1.2 million Jews were killed by these squads in the occupied Soviet territories. In the first two months of operations the victims were mostly men, but beginning in August, the squads killed women and children as well. It was these mass shootings of Jews that initiated the "Final Solution."

THE WILD GRASSES RUSTLE OVER BABI YAR.
THE TREES LOOK OMINOUS,
                    LIKE JUDGES.
HERE ALL THINGS SCREAM SILENTLY,
                    AND, BARING MY HEAD,
SLOWLY I FEEL MYSELF
                    TURNING GRAY.
AND I MYSELF
          AM ONE MASSIVE, SOUNDLESS SCREAM
ABOVE THE THOUSAND THOUSAND BURIED HERE.

YEVGENY YEVTUSHENKO (B. 1933),
RUSSIAN POET

BABI YAR

A few days after the Germans captured Kiev, the capital of the Ukraine, in September 1941, Soviet saboteurs blew up several buildings occupied by German authorities. The Nazis decided that in retaliation, the Jews of Kiev would be killed.

On September 29, signs were posted in Kiev ordering all Jews in the city and its surroundings to appear the next morning, September 29, at the Jewish cemetery. They were to be "resettled," the posters stated; failure to appear was punishable by death.

Thousands of Jews came to the designated place the next morning. They were taken to Babi Yar, a ravine two miles from the city center, and were forced to hand over their valuables and remove their clothes. Groups were then herded into the ravine, where members of a German killing unit shot them.

More than 33,000 Jews were killed at Babi Yar in two days. During the following months, thousands more Jews, as well as partisans, Roma (Gypsies), and Soviet prisoners of war, were executed there. Soviet reports after the war estimated the number of victims at 100,000; the true number may never be known.

In August 1943, as the Red Army advanced, the Nazis returned to Babi Yar to remove the evidence of mass murder. BurN dusters unearthed the thousands of corpses, which were then incinerated.

These exhibits document the beginning of the "Final Solution"—the mass murder of European Jews. As German troops invaded the Soviet Union in 1941, they were accompanied by the Einsatzgruppen, specially trained mobile squads under order to kill all Jews, Gypsies, and Communist party officials. Millions of Jews and countless non-Jews were killed by the Einsatzgruppen, which herded the victims to secluded sites, shot them, and buried them in large pits. Protective walls, here and in other parts of the exhibition, shield young visitors from graphic images of atrocities.

In Babi Yar, on the outskirts of Kiev, Ukraine, 33,771 Jews perished at the hands of the Einsatzgruppen.

THE WARSAW GHETTO UPRISING, PASSOVER 1943

Between July 22 and mid-September 1942, at least 250,000 Jews were deported from the Warsaw ghetto to the Treblinka death camp. For the 60,000 Jews remaining in the ghetto, deportation seemed inevitable.

Zionist, Bundist, and Communist youth groups in the ghetto formed the Jewish Fighting Organization (Żydowska Organizacja Bojowa, or ZOB). Members of the Revisionist party formed another resistance group, the Jewish Military Union (Żydowski Związek Wojskowy, or ZZW).

In January 1943, when the Germans launched a second deportation, the ZOB's commander, Mordecai Anielewicz, called for armed resistance: "Not a single Jew should go to the railroad cars. . . . Our slogan must be: 'Let all be ready to die like human beings.'" After a few days, the deportation came to a halt.

The Germans intended to begin deporting the remaining Jews on April 19, 1943, the eve of Passover. When they entered the ghetto that morning, its streets were deserted; the inhabitants were hiding in bunkers. On that day, the Jewish fighters rose in revolt.

More than 2,000 heavily armed German soldiers and police were backed by tanks and artillery. The 700 to 750 ghetto fighters had a few dozen pistols and hand grenades. Yet in three days of street battles, the Germans were unable to defeat the Jewish combatants.

SS General Jürgen Stroop, the German commander, decided to force out the fighters by burning the ghetto down building by building. Resistance continued until the ghetto was completely destroyed.

The Germans had planned to liquidate the Warsaw ghetto in

April 23, 1943, Mordecai Anielewicz, 24 years old, wrote to Yitzhak Zuckerman, his liaison with the Polish underground:

The dream of my life has become true. Jewish self-defense in the Warsaw ghetto has become a fact. Jewish armed resistance and revenge have become a reality. I have been a witness to the magnificent, heroic struggle of the Jewish fighters.

NAZI DOCUMENTATION

The permanent exhibition explores the scope of Jewish resistance against the Nazis. Armed with only several dozen pistols and hand grenades, a few hundred Jews fought thousands of German soldiers during what has become known as the Warsaw Ghetto uprising of 1943.

In Theresienstadt, workers used hand carts like this to transport the bodies of ghetto prisoners killed by disease and hunger. This manhole cover from the war period was recovered from the Warsaw ghetto. After the uprising, Jewish fighters escaped from the ghetto through the Warsaw sewer system. The cobblestones once paved Chlodna Street inside the Warsaw ghetto.

Railroad cars, such as this one, were used to
transport Jews from camps and ghettos to six
killing centers in Poland. As many as 100 people
were packed into a single car without sanitation,
food, or water; many did not survive the trip.

The exhibition's circulation path takes visitors through this rail car, which sits on rails taken from the Treblinka station. One of six Nazi death camps, Treblinka was used primarily to gas inhabitants of the Warsaw ghetto. Unsuspecting victims, destined for the gas chambers, were told that they were being resettled in the east. Accordingly, they brought with them to Auschwitz luggage and personal effects which were then seized by Nazi guards.

These Hungarian Jews, photographed by an SS camp officer, had no idea what awaited them as they entered Auschwitz-Birkenau in western Poland in 1944. As they disembarked from the trains, SS officers conducted a selection of new arrivals. The sick, the elderly, pregnant women, women with young children, and children too young to work were sent immediately to the gas chambers. Those deemed capable of work were assigned to slave labor.

The Nazis seized all of the personal belongings of camp inmates. Pictured here are umbrellas, prayer shawls, and artificial limbs and leg braces confiscated by the Nazis at Auschwitz.

WE ARE THE SHOES, WE ARE THE LAST WITNESSES.
WE ARE SHOES FROM GRANDCHILDREN AND GRANDFATHERS,
FROM PRAGUE, PARIS, AND AMSTERDAM,
AND BECAUSE WE ARE ONLY MADE OF FABRIC AND LEATHER
AND NOT OF BLOOD AND FLESH, EACH ONE OF US AVOIDED THE HELLFIRE.

MOSES SCHULSTEIN (1911–1981),
YIDDISH POET

Before Jews were gassed at killing centers such as Majdanek, Treblinka, and Auschwitz, the SS seized all of their possessions. These shoes were confiscated from prisoners in Majdanek.

Nearly all prisoners selected for labor were registered and many were photographed upon arrival at the camps. Since most Jews were immediately sent to their death, neither registration forms nor photographs exist for the majority of victims.

Overleaf: Visitors pass under this gate, a cast taken from the original entrance to the Auschwitz death camp, inscribed with the ironic phrase Arbeit Macht Frei.

THE CONCENTRATION CAMP UNIVERSE

In the early years of the Nazi regime, concentration camps held mainly political prisoners. As Germany prepared for war, major camps were established to supply slave labor for war production. In 1942 the concentration camps held 100,000 inmates, and by 1943, 224,000. This number almost doubled by 1944, to reach 524,000. In January 1945 there were 714,000 concentration camp inmates, more than 200,000 of them women.

The vast network of thousands of camps throughout Europe eventually included internment camps, prisoner-of-war camps, work-education camps, slave-labor camps, "youth protection" camps, camps for conscript laborers, transit camps, and killing centers. Over 300 camps housed only women. Between 1939 and 1945, tens of thousands of prisoners died in camps from exposure, starvation, disease, physical abuse, and shooting.

Within eight months of the Wannsee Conference of January 1942, six killing centers were in operation. Most deportees sent to them were gassed on arrival. More than 3 million people, primarily Jews, died in these killing centers.

"ARBEIT MACHT FREI"

The inscription over the main gate to Auschwitz, "Arbeit macht frei" ("Work will make you free"), was a cynical deceit, suggesting that inmates who worked would eventually be released. In reality, inmates who could no longer work were deemed useless and sent to the gas chambers. Prisoners who marched through this gate, worked in the camp's slave-labor factories, and returned each day, often collapsed from exhaustion, illness, and abuse.

This arch is a replica from the entrance to the Auschwitz concentration camp. During mass in possession of the State Museum at Auschwitz, Oświęcim, Poland.

The Nazis tattooed concentration camp inmates with serial numbers.

Visitors to this audio theater hear Auschwitz survivors relate their experiences of terror, brutality, and despair.

VOICES FROM AUSCHWITZ

This audio theater presents the spoken memories of Auschwitz survivors.

VOICES FROM AUSCHWITZ

This audio theater presents the spoken memories of Auschwitz survivors.

In 1941, when Auschwitz I became too small to accommodate the flood of prisoners, Auschwitz II-Birkenau was built and became the largest of the Nazi killing centers. This reconstructed barracks, taken from Auschwitz-Birkenau, housed Jews deported from the Theresienstadt ghetto in Czechoslovakia.

Prisoners slept five or six to a bed on three-level bunks. A single barracks housed as many as 500 inmates.

Overleaf: The Museum commissioned Polish sculptor Jan Stobierski to re-create the scale model of the killing process at Auschwitz which has been on display at the Auschwitz Museum for many years. The model documents the fate of Nazi victims who had no idea that they were being led to their death.

KILLING CENTERS

In 1941 and 1942 the Nazis established six killing centers, at Auschwitz-Birkenau, Majdanek, Chelmno, Belzec, Sobibor, and Treblinka. Auschwitz-Birkenau and Majdanek also functioned as concentration camps; the other four were exclusively death camps. All were located near railroad lines in Poland. The primary method of killing was asphyxiation by carbon monoxide or Zyklon B (prussic acid) gas. An exact count of the dead is not possible. Estimates vary, but there is consensus on the range of the number of death camp victims.

CHELMNO

Gassings began on December 8, 1941, and ended 22 months later in this town west of Lodz. The victims were herded into vans that were then hermetically sealed; engine exhaust was routed into the vans until those inside were dead. Between 150,000 and 320,000 people died at Chelmno, most of them Jews. Among those gassed were 5,000 Roma (Gypsies) and thousands of Poles and Soviet prisoners of war.

BELZEC

From March to December 1942, between 550,000 and 590,000 Jews, and about 2,000 Roma, were gassed at Belzec. As at Sobibor and Treblinka, carbon monoxide gas produced by diesel engines was the killing agent.

SOBIBOR

Over a period of 18 months, 200,000 Jews and possibly more Jews died at Sobibor in carbon monoxide gas chambers. Three hundred prisoners escaped during a camp revolt in October 1943; at the war's end, 50 of them were still alive.

TREBLINKA

During 14 months beginning in July 1942, from 750,000 to 870,000 Jews were killed at Treblinka by a staff of 120 Ukrainian volunteers and 30 SS personnel. Most of the latter were veterans of the Nazi euthanasia program. Fewer than 100 prisoners managed to escape from the camp.

MAJDANEK

From 360,000 to 500,000 people died in Majdanek, located outside Lublin. Approximately 40 percent of the prisoners who arrived there were Jews. About 100,000 Jews were killed in Majdanek's gas chambers or died of starvation, exhaustion, exposure, and mistreatment.

AUSCHWITZ-BIRKENAU

Between 1.1 million and 1.25 million people were murdered in the largest of the Nazi killing centers, most of them in the gas chambers of Auschwitz-Birkenau. They included tens of thousands of Poles, 20,000 Roma, from 10,000 to 20,000 Soviet prisoners of war, and about 1 million Jews.

2. GASSING

When the victims had taken off their clothes, they were herded into an underground gas chamber, disguised with fake shower heads as a shower room. Women and children, who were usually the majority, went in first. As soon as the chamber was filled with people, sealed, and locked, SS guards poured Zyklon B pellets in through special vents in the roof. The pellets fell to the floor, releasing their deadly gas. Most of the victims died within a few minutes. After about 20 minutes, when all were dead, ventilators expelled the poisonous air.

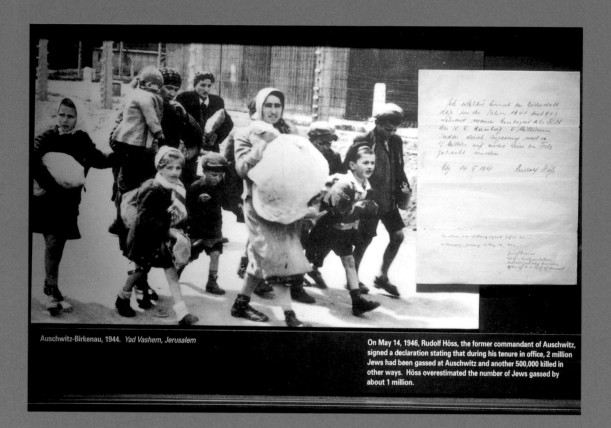

Auschwitz-Birkenau, 1944. *Yad Vashem, Jerusalem*

On May 14, 1946, Rudolf Höss, the former commandant of Auschwitz, signed a declaration stating that during his tenure in office, 2 million Jews had been gassed at Auschwitz and another 500,000 killed in other ways. Höss overestimated the number of Jews gassed by about 1 million.

This affidavit, signed by Auschwitz commandant Rudolf Hoess, states that two million inmates were gassed and 500,000 were killed in other ways at Auschwitz. Historians now believe that Hoess overestimated the number of victims gassed by about one million.

Facing page: A high-ranking Nazi officer at Mauthausen, the major concentration camp in Austria.

▲ Brutal punishments took place every day in the camps. Here, two guards beat a prisoner in front of his fellow inmates at Poniatowa, a subcamp of the Majdanek concentration camp. *Jewish Historical Institute, Warsaw*

▲ Concentration camps often received visits from major Nazi party and government officials. Here, a high-ranking SS official inspects construction work at the Mauthausen concentration camp. 1941? *Musée de la Résistance et la Déportation, Besançon, France*

▼ Initiation into concentration camp life was degrading for women, who had to undress in fro of SS guards. These newly arrived Hungarian Jewish women have just had their hair shorn Wearing camp uniforms, they are entering the women's section of Auschwitz-Birkenau. May–June 1944. *Yad Vashem, Jerusalem*

Below: Replica of a crematorium in the Austrian concentration camp of Mauthausen.

Right: Barbed wire fence post from Auschwitz. Between them a quotation from Elie Wiesel's book *Night*.

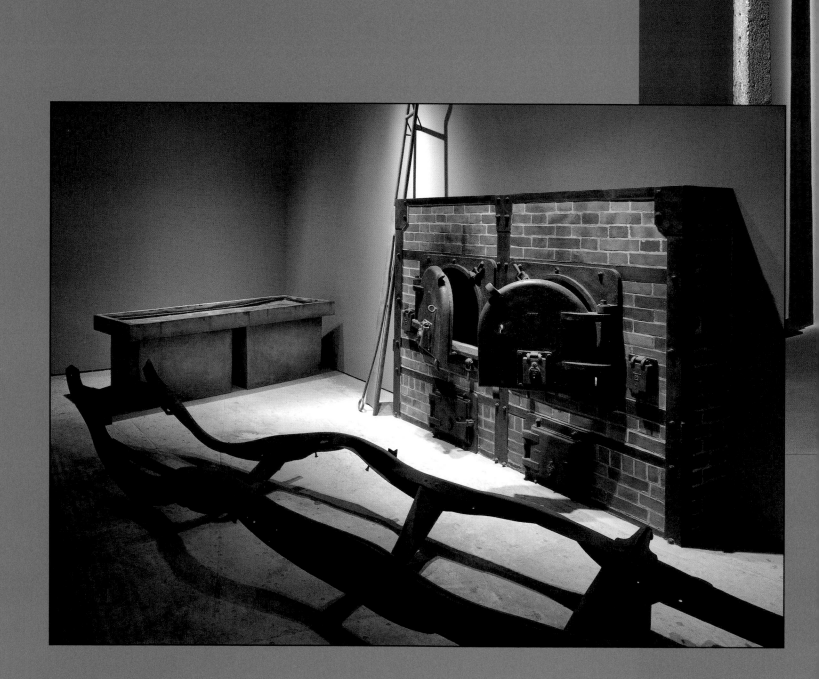

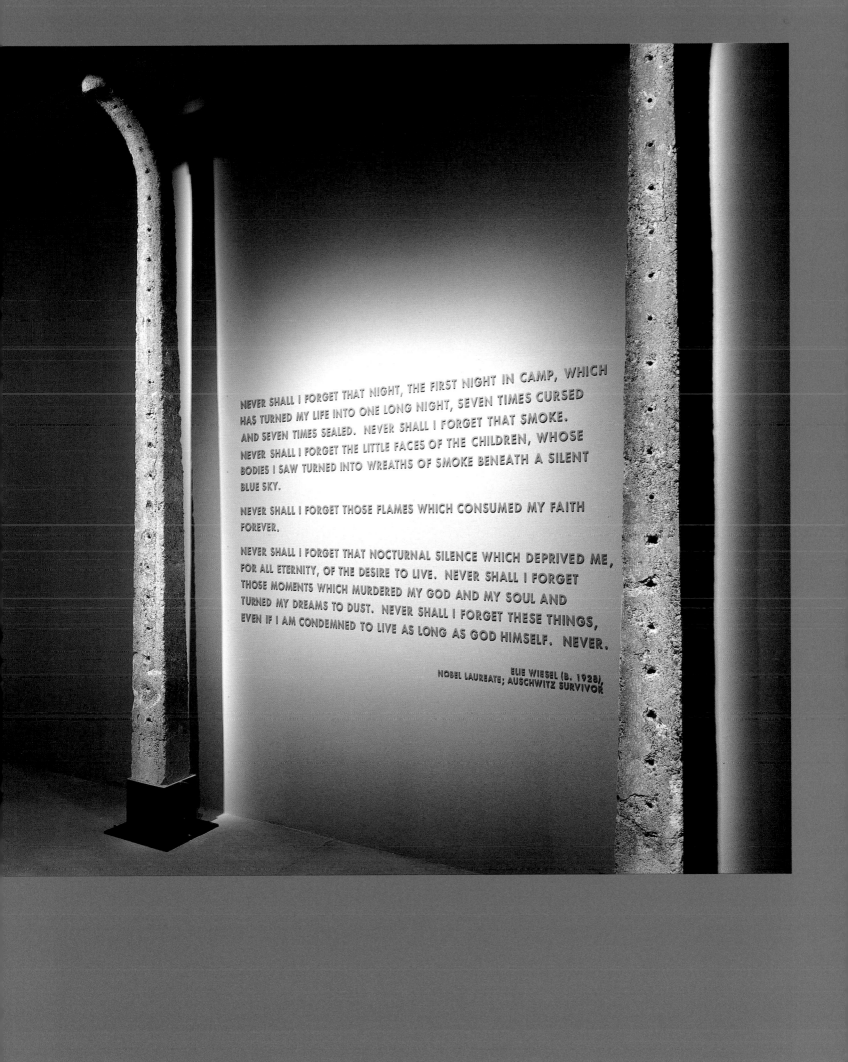

What have you done? Hark, thy brother's blood cries out to me from the ground!

Genesis 4:10

The Tower of Faces.

In the winter of 1942, Catholic democrats of the Polish underground formed the Rada Pomocy Zydom, the Council for Aid to Jews, code-named the Zegota. At great personal risks, members of the Zegota, aided by other Jewish and Polish resistance groups, provided help to 4,000 Jews by supplying false documents, assisting in escapes, providing safe havens, and offering foster care to more than 2,500 Jewish children.

Most non-Jews in occupied Europe did nothing to help or hinder the Nazi genocide. A small number, however, risked their lives to help Jews escape death in the Holocaust. These exhibits on the second and final floors of the permanent exhibition tell the stories of rescuers in Poland, Italy, Bulgaria, Hungary, and other countries.

Acting on behalf of the World Refugee Board, Raoul Wallenberg, a Swedish diplomat based in Budapest, led the most extensive rescue effort. By issuing these Schutzpasses ("protective passports") signed with his initial, Wallenberg saved thousands of Hungarian Jews from deportation to Auschwitz. Wallenberg was seen for the last time with Soviet troops in 1945; a decade later, Soviet authorities admitted that he had been arrested and claimed that he died in prison in 1947. However, alleged sightings of Wallenberg continued into the 1980s. His fate remains a mystery.

RAOUL WALLENBERG
1941-1912

Roundups and executions of the Jews of Budapest began immediately after Germany installed a puppet Hungarian government, led by the fascist Arrow Cross party, on October 16, 1944. In the following days, about 600 Jews were killed. *Bundesarchiv Koblenz, Germany*

This photograph is believed to show Raoul Wallenberg negotiating with Hungarian policemen in Budapest to prevent the deportation of Jewish men to slave-labor camps in Austria. Wallenberg is at the right, with his hands clasped behind his back. At his right, a deportee holds a Swedish "protective passport." November 1944. *Tom Veres, Photographer*

Raoul Wallenberg established his headquarters in the Swedish embassy at Budapest. November 26, 1944. *Tom Veres, Photographer*

By giving these Jews Swedish "protective passports" at railroad station, Raoul Wallenberg saved them from dep labor camps in Austria. November 1944. *Tom Veres, Pho*

Portrait of Raoul Wallenberg donated by the National Swedish Art Museums, Stockholm

Raoul Wallenberg issued thousands of "protective passports" (Schutz-*pässe*) signed with his initial, W. to shield the Jews of Budapest from deportation. In them was a guarantee that the holder would emigrate

In 1953, the Israeli parliament directed the Yad Vashem Remembrance Authority to establish a memorial to "the Righteous among the Nations who risked their lives to save Jews." The rescuers' wall at the Museum pays tribute to more than 10,000 individuals identified by Yad Vashem's research through December 1993. While the stories of some rescuers are highlighted—like that of Joop Westerweel—all of the men, women and children listed on this wall demonstrated tremendous courage and compassion, though they regarded their acts as no more than expressions of ordinary decency.

Joop Westerweel (1899–1944)

Westerweel was a schoolteacher in the town of Bilthoven. When deportations of Dutch Jews began in 1942, he helped organize an underground movement that hid young Jews and aided them to leave the country. They were smuggled out to Belgium, then to France, and from there to Switzerland or Spain. The Germans captured Westerweel and subjected him to severe torture, but he did not reveal his network of contacts. He was executed on August 11, 1944. The underground group continued its activities, smuggling from 150 to 200 Jews out of the Netherlands.

Photo: Yad Vashem, Jerusalem

Denmark rescued virtually all of its Jews. In 1943,
when Danes learned of plans to deport Jews,
Danish political leaders, the clergy, and ordinary
citizens coordinated efforts to smuggle Jews by
boat to neutral Sweden. This boat and others like it
were used by a group code-named the "Helsingor
Sewing Club" to carry twelve to fourteen Jews per
trip to safety.

This is Nazi Brutality

RADIO BERLIN.--IT IS OFFICIALLY ANNOUNCED:-
MEN OF LIDICE - CZECHOSLOVAKIA - HAVE BEEN SHOT:
THE WOMEN DEPORTED TO A CONCENTRATION CAMP:
THE CHILDREN SENT TO APPROPRIATE CENTERS-- THE
NAME OF THE VILLAGE WAS IMMEDIATELY ABOLISHED.
6/11/42/115P

The Czech parachutist Jan Kubiš threw the bomb that fatally wounded Reinhard Heydrich. Prague, Czechoslovakia, June 18, 1942. *Czechoslovak News Agency, Prague*

Jan Kubiš's partner, the Czech parachutist Josef Gabčík, attempted to shoot Reinhard Heydrich, but his submachine gun jammed. Prague, Czechoslovakia, June 18, 1942. *Czechoslovak News Agency, Prague*

The reprisals for Heydrich's assassination included the burning and razing of Lidice. June 1942. *Czechoslovak News Agency, Prague*

German policemen shot almost 200 men of Lidice on June 10, 1942. That same day, Jewish inmates of the Theresienstadt ghetto were brought to Lidice and forced to bury the dead. *Library of Congress, Washington, D.C.*

▲ These identity cards belonged to men of Lidice who were killed on June 10, 1942. *On loan from*

Lidice had been a mining
lamp was one of those

This section of the exhibition explores Jewish resistance to Nazi persecution. Between 1941 and 1943, Jews formed underground resistance movements in nearly 100 ghettos. Jewish partisans fought Nazi Germany and its collaborators throughout Europe. In Auschwitz, Jewish concentration camp prisoners managed to blow up a crematorium. In Sobibor and Treblinka, they organized escapes.

Overleaf: These tree trunks were taken from Rudniki forest which sheltered the largest group of Jewish partisans in Soviet-occupied territory. Their units around the city of Vilna derailed hundreds of German trains and killed more than 3,000 Nazi soldiers.

Bruskina was hanged with two other partisans

JEWISH RESISTANCE FIGHTERS

TREES FROM THE RUDNIKI FOREST I[...]

...bruary 1944, these three Jewish partisans were photographed in the
...ckow forest, near Warsaw. They are (from left) Gabriel Prushchnk,
...ub Puttermilch, and Janek Bielak. Bielak fell in the Warsaw Polish
...rising of August 1944.

This photograph shows Dudo Montiljo, a Bosnian Jew.
In 1943 he joined the Yugoslav partisans, led by Josip Tito,
who were fighting Germany.

In Croatia, Jews fought with Yugoslav partisans against
Germany and the fascist Ustaša regime. These Browning
and Mauser pistols belonged to the Jewish partisans
Dudo Montiljo, Lavoslav Kadelburg, and Leo Geršcovic.
Federation of Jewish Communities in Yugoslavia, Belgrade

Egon Novak (left) and Oskar Wertheimer (third from left)
were among the 1,566 Jewish partisans who fought in the
Slovak national uprising, an attempt to overthrow Jozef
Tiso's pro-Nazi puppet government. Beth Hatefutsoth
Museum of the Diaspora, Tel Aviv, Israel

...his cap and satchel for holding maps and bread belonged to Jacob
...ltaras, a Jewish member of Tito's Yugoslav Communist resistance

These weapon[...]
a German[...]
uprising b[...]

LIBERATION: ENCOUNTER

During Germany's military collapse, the converging armies of the Allies and the Soviets liberated the concentration camps that lay in their path. The liberations were not a primary objective; they were a by-product of the goal, which was to defeat Germany and its allies.

The first liberation took place in July 1944, when four Soviet divisions entered the Majdanek concentration camp near Lublin, Poland. The following autumn and winter, Soviet forces liberated more camps, in Estonia, Latvia, Lithuania, and Poland. Auschwitz was freed on January 27, 1945.

Also in 1945, British, Canadian, American, and Free French units liberated concentration camps in Germany. As they advanced from the west, American divisions freed Dora-Mittelbau, Buchenwald, Flossenbürg, Dachau, and Mauthausen. In northern Germany, British forces liberated Bergen-Belsen and Neuengamme. A few weeks before Germany surrendered, Soviet divisions liberated Stutthof, Sachsenhausen, and Ravensbrück.

Although the Germans had attempted to evacuate the camps, they still housed thousands of starved and diseased prisoners. The combat-hardened Allied and Soviet troops were unprepared for what they encountered: heaps of rotting human corpses, and barracks filled with dead and dying prisoners. The stench of death was everywhere.

MAUTHHAUSEN CONCENTRATION CAMP AT LIBERATION

LIBERATION AFTERMAT

BRITISH ARMY: BERGEN-BELSEN

NAZI WAR FLAG

When Soviet, British, and American troops liberated the concentration camps, they were stunned by the evidence of Nazi mass murder and by the sight of tens of thousands of survivors ravaged by starvation and disease.

During the Nuremburg Trial, the International Military Tribunal representing the Allied nations prosecuted Nazi leaders for conspiracy to wage a war of aggression, for war crimes, and for crimes against humanity. This last charge dealt specifically with genocide of the Jews. Visitors may use ear phones to listen to actual recordings of the proceeding at Nuremburg.

...laková, born May 28, 1930; deported to Auschwitz, October 23 or 28, 1944; survived.

Robert Bondy, born May 1, 1932; deported to Auschwitz, October 8, 1944

Ilona Weissová, born March 6, 1932; deported to Auschwitz, May 15, 1944

Eva Kohnová, born April 29, 1930; deported to Auschwitz, May 18, 1944

Helga Weissová, born November 10, 1929; deported to Auschwitz, October 5, 1944; survived

Eva Brunnerová, born August 27, 1933; deported to Auschwitz, October 4, 1944.

Helena Mandlová, born May 21, 1930; deported to Auschwitz, December 18, 1943

Approximately 1.5 million children under the age of 15 died during the Holocaust. These are paintings made by children in the Theresienstadt ghetto near Prague. Of the 15,000 children who passed through Theresienstadt, only a few hundred survived.

After Israel, the United States was the most favored destination of Holocaust survivors, but legislation to expedite the admission of Jewish displaced persons was slow in coming. In 1948, Congress finally passed a bill permitting the immigration of 50,000 European refugees per year until 1952. However, the bill included severe restrictions that effectively excluded many Jews. By the time the bill was amended in 1950, most Jewish displaced persons had settled in Israel.

A NEW WORLD

After Israel, the most favored destination of Jewish Holocaust survivors was the United States. But legislation to expedite the admission of Jewish displaced persons (DPs) was slow in coming.

Between December 22, 1945, and June 1947, a total of 22,950 DPs were admitted into the United States, of whom two-thirds were Jewish. President Harry S. Truman favored a liberal immigration policy toward DPs, but congressional action was needed to raise the strict immigration quotas.

The American Jewish community lobbied for such action. In 1948, Congress finally passed a bill allowing 50,000 European refugees to immigrate per year until 1952. Its restrictions were so severe, however, that President Truman called the law "flagrantly discriminatory against Jews." Congress amended the law in 1950, but by the following year, most of the Jewish DPs in Europe had gone to the newly established state of Israel.

By 1952, 137,450 Jewish refugees had settled in the United States. The amended 1948 law served as a turning point in American immigration policy, establishing a precedent for later refugee crises.

After the war, many thousands of Jewish survivors, unable or unwilling to return to their homes, were forced to live in displaced person camps in Europe under sometimes harsh conditions. Thousands more attempted to enter Palestine illegally, despite the British ban on large-scale Jewish immigration. Finally, in November 1947, the United Nations General Assembly voted to partition Palestine into a Jewish and an Arab state. In 1948, the nation of Israel was formed under this Declaration of Independence.

Overleaf: The final element in the exhibition is a film in which survivors recount their experiences of loss, suffering, and anguish, as well as rescue, resistance, compassion, and hope. Amphitheater walls are faced with stone from Jerusalem.

THE VALUES AND PRINCIPLES
OF A LIVING MUSEUM

COMMITMENT TO HISTORICAL TRUTH

In its endeavor to create an exhibition that would in itself serve as historical evidence, the planning team developed an almost fanatic commitment to historical truth. All textual explanations were vetted by renowned Holocaust scholars, all exhibits carefully checked for authenticity. The slightest doubt about the accuracy of the caption of a photograph, or about the provenance of an artifact, led immediately to its disqualification. This quest for truthfulness and proven authenticity helped give the exhibition a very high degree of credibility. Any mistakes would have left the Museum open to critical attacks against its historical reliability.

Sometimes members of the team carried this pursuit of historical accuracy to great lengths. When the Museum received the red boxcar as a present from the then-Communist Polish government, with written attestation that the car had been used to transport Jews from the Warsaw ghetto to their death in the gas chambers of Treblinka, some staff members believed that a statement issued by a Communist government could not be considered reliable. They began researching the provenance of the car with the help of the director of a railway museum in Germany, trying to determine whether in German documents relating to the deportation of Jews from Warsaw the serial number of this particular car could be found. Since the research led to no conclusive results, the historian who was responsible for writing labels and captions insisted that the label for the car be worded accordingly, explaining that "the walkway goes through a 15-ton freight car, one of several types that were used to deport Jews," rather than "this car was used to deport . . ."

In another case, members of the planning team questioned whether one could include in the exhibition the affidavit of Rudolph Hoess, in which he stated that during his tenure as commandant of Auschwitz two million inmates had been gassed and half a million more had perished in the camp in other ways. Today historians believe that the total number of inmates who perished in Auschwitz was a million and a half, or even less. Obviously, Hoess, who wrote the affidavit in a prison cell in Nuremberg, gave an estimate not based on statistical research. However, it was a historic fact that he wrote this admission of guilt of his free will. The affidavit was written in the presence of a member of the American team at the Nuremberg war crime trials who interrogated Hoess, and it was this eyewitness who donated the historic document to the Museum after having kept it for almost fifty years in his private archive. Even so, some staff members were afraid

Railway car donated by the Polish Government

Opposite: A cast of the wall that stands in the Remu synagogue's cemetery in Krakow. A memorial to those who died in the Holocaust, the wall was built with fragments of tombstones broken by the Nazis for use elsewhere.

153

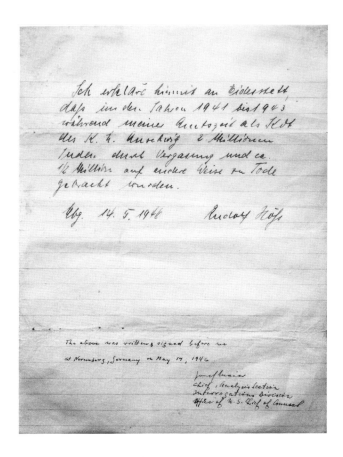

Affidavit by Auschwitz camp commander Rudolf Hoess overstating the number of people killed in the camp.

someone might accuse the Museum of overstating the number of Auschwitz victims. Eventually, after heated debates, it was decided that the documents be included in the exhibition with a caption quoting the correct statistic.

In yet another case, stout concern for the historical reliability of the exhibition combined with ideological fervor and insufficient research led to public embarrassment. A young historian, who was involved in writing the text panel for the exhibition segment devoted to the rescue of the Jewish population in Denmark, insisted that it be stated that poor Jews who could not afford to pay the passage to Sweden were left behind. Not finding documentary evidence about the matter, he reasoned that since it was known that the boatmen who carried the Jews to Sweden received payment, and some Jews remained in Denmark, obviously those were left behind because they were unable to pay. He thought it was important to state this explicitly, because otherwise the exhibition would be presenting the Danish rescuers in an unwarranted saintly way, and thereby distort history. A knowledgeable leader of the Danish Jewish community found the statement false and offensive. He explained that nobody was left behind because of poverty; some could not or did not want to go because they were too old or too sick and others did not believe that the Germans were about to arrest and deport them. The Danish panel was added to the list of post-opening textual corrections.

Even though its planners strove for high standards of factual accuracy, the exhibition can by no means profess historical objectivity: no historical narrative can. Composing a narrative means organizing a seemingly chaotic multitude of historic events into a sequential, and perhaps causal, pattern. Thus every historic period lends itself to many different interpretations.

Several years ago, Holocaust scholars were involved in a worldwide controversy about the correct reading of the historic events that led to the annihilation of European Jews in the Holocaust. The "intentionalists" regarded the annihilation of the Jews as an undertaking planned, initiated, and directed by Adolf Hitler, the execution of a decision that was made long before it was actually carried out. The "functionalists," on the other hand, regarded the decision to kill the Jews as having evolved over time, mainly as the result of power struggles among the major bureaucratic power centers within the hierarchic structure of the Third Reich. Mainstream Holocaust research eventually reconciled the two seemingly contradictory views, and there is no way to determine which of them was more objective. More recently, another worldwide controversy among Holocaust scholars, unusually referred to as the *Historikerstreit* (struggle among the historians) broke out as the result of attempts at revisionist reinterpretation of Holocaust history by right-wing German historians, who are trying in various ways to relativize the enormity of the crimes of the Third Reich. One could easily conceive of two different, and partly contradictory, narratives, one based on an "intentionalist," and the other on a "functionalist" interpretation of Holocaust history; or one based on the revisionist view that presents Nazi crimes as commensurate with acts of mass destruction committed during the war by the Allies and later by the Soviet regime, and the other based on the view that the Holocaust cannot be compared to any other event in human history. All narratives could be based on the very same factual findings and still present entirely different interpretations.

The exhibition of the United States Holocaust Memorial Museum is based on a narrative essentially reflecting the point of view of the Jewish victim, even though it tries to include in its presentation, more than any other Holocaust Museum in the world, the plight of all non-Jewish victim groups. Clearly, Holocaust museums built by the German or the French government would be based on entirely different narratives. The reason why neither Germany nor France have major Holocaust museums — only small memorial museums on the sites of former concentration camps—may have something to do with the difficulty of composing a narrative that would be acceptable both to their respective nations and to public opinion in the rest of the Western world. The site museum of Auschwitz, conceived and created by Communist Poland, based its interpretation of Holocaust history on a narrative that tried to present the victims of the Auschwitz gas chambers as Polish anti-fascists, hiding the fact that they were killed regardless of their political leanings only because they were Jews.

Though there is no such thing as objective historiography, and there is no end to the controversies among Holocaust scholars over questions of interpretation, there is general agreement on the basic facts. To quote the eminent German Holocaust historian Hans Mommsen: ". . . the actual course of events has now been largely established . . . at most there is marginal controversy about the exact number of victims." (*From Weimer to Auschwitz*, Princeton: Princeton University Press, 1991) The planning team of the Museum tried to stick to the "established course of events" and to remain in line with the views of mainstream Holocaust scholarship in the United States and Israel.

Danish Jews escaping to Sweden.

Above: Members of the Jewish Council in Ghetto Kovno with Chairman Elchanan Elkes (center), who supported the anti-Nazi underground within the Ghetto.

Center: Adam Czerniakow, chairman of the Warsaw Ghetto Jewish Council, who committed suicide when requested to deliver children for deportation to death camps.

Below: Chaim Rumkowki, Chairman of the Jewish Council in Ghetto Lodz, speaking to Heinrich Himmler, head of the SS.

This position did not always save the planning team from dealing with controversial issues however. There was the problem, for example, of how and in what light to present the historic role of the *Judenraete* (the Jewish Councils) and the Jewish police in the ghettos. Until very recently, the dominant trend was to stereotype the Jewish Councils and the police in all ghettos as evil collaborators with the Nazi authorities who assisted actively in the annihilation of the Jewish population. This view was powerfully represented by such eminent historians as Hannah Arendt and Raul Hilberg. Several years ago, however, mainstream Holocaust scholarship adopted a more discriminating approach, realizing that there was a wide spectrum of behavior patterns, from outright collaboration with the Germans, which was the case in most ghettos, to clandestine collaboration with the Jewish underground, which was the case in some. The planning team went along with the more balanced and now generally accepted approach that postulates that every case and every personality has to be judged on its own merits. There also was the widespread trend of stereotyping the Jews as being "led like sheep to the slaughterhouse," and of minimizing the scope of Jewish resistance against the Nazis. Here, too, the team rejected obsolete stereotypes and adopted a more sophisticated position, trying to do justice to the many manifestations of Jewish heroism in the resistance against the Nazi murderers—from the fighters of the Warsaw ghetto uprising, to Rosa Robota, the Jewish girl who was hanged for smuggling into Auschwitz the explosives that were used to blow up one of the gas chambers, to the Jewish martyrs of the armed resistance in occupied France. It was this approach that also motivated the Museum to choose the story of the Kovno ghetto as the theme of one of its very first special exhibitions, Kovno being an exceptional example of cooperation by the leaders of the Jewish Councils and the commandant of the ghetto police with the Jewish underground.

Cautiously navigating its way around the complexities of Holocaust history, the planning team meticulously kept away

Above: Heroes of the resistance movement: Haika Grosman, Bialystok; Rosa Robota, Auschwitz; Mordecai Anielewicz, commander of the Warsaw Ghetto uprising.

Below: Jewish partisans pose in Vilna on day of the city's liberation, from left to right: Rushka Korczak, Abba Kovner, Vitka Kempner.

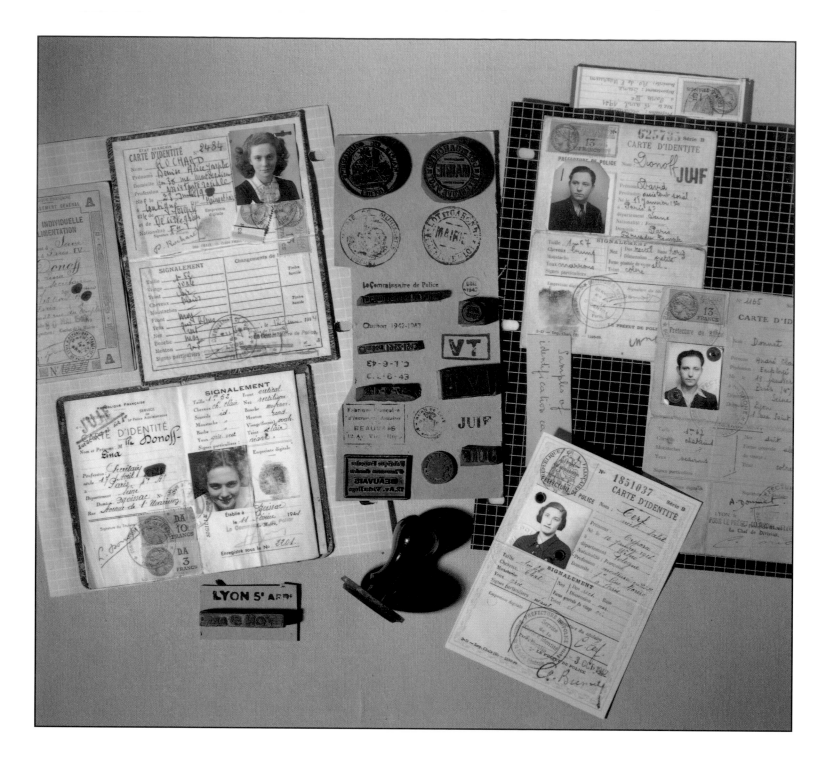

Forged documents and the rubber stamps used to make them by Jewish resistance members.

from Holocaust victim statistics. There has never been agreement among scholars about the number of people who perished in the Holocaust. While it is customary to quote the symbolic figure of 6 million Jewish Holocaust victims, scholarly estimates vary between 5.1 million and slightly over 6 million. The *Encyclopedia of the Holocaust* (New York: Macmillan, 1990) quotes 5.86 million. The planning team did not want to adopt any of the varying estimates, nor was it able to embark on a project of statistical research of its own. It therefore refrained from mentioning figures altogether.

Victims statistics relating to other major victim groups are even more vague and divergent. In the case of Poles and Soviet prisoners of war murdered by the Nazis, it is difficult to define who should be categorized as Holocaust victims and who as war casualties in the national struggle against the German invaders. Another reason the Museum kept away from figures was the sensitivity of the issue, mainly in Polish and Gypsy communities, where some believe the number of their victims defines the magnitude of their tragedy. Not only are there no reliable figures available about Polish and Gypsy victims, but the whole attitude of quantitatively measuring and comparing national tragedies can be felt as demeaning and showing lack of respect for the individual victim.

The planning team knew its task was to present the Holocaust as an unprecedented breakdown of civilization whose severity could and should not be perceived in terms of any comparative national statistics.

INCLUDING ALL VICTIMS

At the very beginning, there were differences of opinion on whether the Museum should also depict the fate of non-Jewish Holocaust victims. But the 1979 President's Commission on the Holocaust mandated the inclusion of non-Jewish victims and recommended in its report that "the Museum incorporate displays on Poles, Gypsies and other exterminated groups." This was a wise approach, since to portray the Holocaust truthfully, the Museum had to present it in its totality, in its full historical context, which did not solely consist of the mass murder of the Jews. Moreover, it was impossible to emphasize the universal, human significance of the Holocaust without being inclusive of all victims.

Although most of the exhibits relate to the Jewish victims, the exhibition also includes material about the Poles, the Sinti and Roma (Gypsies), Soviet prisoners of war, the handicapped, homosexuals, Jehovah's Witnesses, Freemasons, and political dissidents. In fact, the most difficult part of the search for artifacts was the effort to find exhibits relating to the non-Jewish victim groups, and the planning team devoted much energy to this endeavor.

With the help of two experts on Gypsy ethnography, a Gypsy wagon was found and brought from Czechoslovakia to be displayed on the upper exhibition floor. The Museum also obtained the violin of a Gypsy musician who was executed by the Germans and a traditional Gypsy woman's dress. An audiovisual program on the fate of the Gypsies

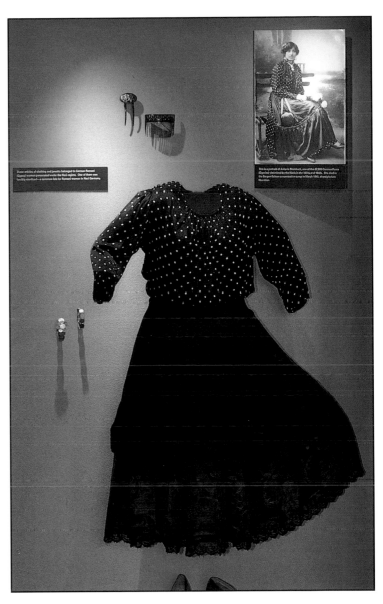

Gypsy artifacts from Czechoslovakia.

was produced and included in the exhibition. During the incubation years of the exhibition, American Gypsy leaders, one of whom was a member of the Museum Council, kept demanding emphatically that the exhibition present the persecution of the Gypsies in the Holocaust appropriately, not trusting the assurances given by staff as to its adherence to the principle of inclusiveness. The tension that accom-

Images from Poland, from top to bottom: execution of Catholic priest; Irena Sendler and Zofia Kossak-Szczucka, heroic members of Zegota, the illegal Polish organization that helped Jews during the Holocaust; coffins of anti-Jewish pogrom victims in Kielce, 1946.

panied these demands faded away with the opening of the Museum, when it became obvious that the Museum had not ignored the plight of the Gypsies.

Another group anxious to make sure that their victims were appropriately included in the exhibition was the Polish community in the United States and Canada. One of their eminent clerical personalities, Father John Pawlikowski of Chicago, was a member of the United States Holocaust Memorial Council and the Content Committee until after the opening of the Museum. In the meetings of the Committee, he tactfully represented the Polish cause and made sure that the exhibition planners would not forget the sufferings of the Poles under Nazi occupation. In line with the principle of inclusiveness, the planners designed a most impressive exhibition segment on anti-Polish atrocities perpetrated by German soldiers, showing the faces of Polish citizens in the last minutes before their execution, and German soldiers in the act of executing them. A tree stump that served as the marker of a mass grave was brought from the Palmiry forest, near Warsaw, where Germans had killed thousands of Poles in pursuit of their declared policy to annihilate the political, intellectual, and clerical elite of Poland. The marker is displayed on the background of a large picture of the Palmiry forest, with Germans leading Poles to their death. In the section devoted to the rescue of Jews by non-Jews, a segment was included on "Zegota," a group of Polish Catholics who risked their lives to assist and save Jews. Also, a large panel with mug shots of concentration camp prisoners contains mainly photographs of Poles.

Even so, some American-Polish and Canadian-Polish organizations continued aggressively to voice their dissatisfaction with the way the Museum was dealing with the Polish aspect of the Holocaust. One of their complaints was about the inclusion in the exhibition of a segment on the 1946 pogrom in Kielce, in which forty-two Jews were killed by Poles, and which triggered the almost total exodus of Jews from postwar Poland. They demanded that the segment be removed. This demand was voiced neither by Father Pawlikowski nor by the Polish embassy, which was always in close and friendly contact with the Museum. Naturally the pictures of the Kielce pogrom, which depicted a very important event in the direct aftermath of the Holocaust, remained in place.

The Jehovah's Witnesses were yet another group whose inclusion in the exhibition posed difficulties. In this case the problem lay in the extreme scarcity of exhibits. To help the Museum tell the story of the group, a Jehovah's Witness volunteer assisted the planning team for years in its efforts to obtain material for the exhibition. He also arranged video interviews with Jehovah's Witnesses, documenting their and their families' experience during the Holocaust. Unfortunately, in spite of his devoted research, not much material was found.

The United States Holocaust Memorial Museum was the first Holocaust museum to present, in the framework of an encompassing portrayal of the Holocaust, material on the victimization of homosexuals. A gay academician continues to assist the Museum in securing exhibits and eyewitness testimonies about the persecution of

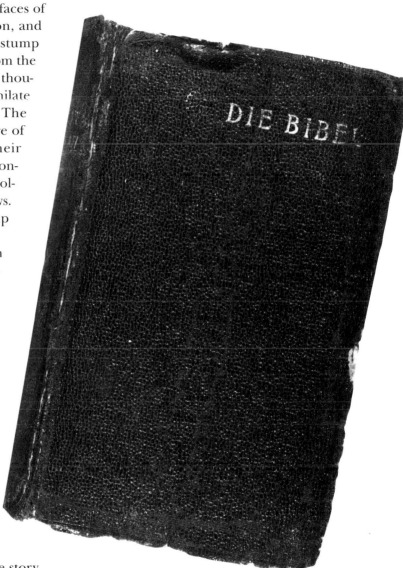

Bible kept by Jehovah's Witness who died in Sachsenhaussen concentration camp.

homosexuals during the Holocaust. Unfortunately, little material was obtained, mainly because until quite recently few German homosexuals had come out. Even so, most organized gay groups came to regard the Museum as pursuing the right course of action. During the opening week, gay activists organized across the street from the Museum a vigil in memory of the homosexual Holocaust victims, and a group of gay businessmen undertook to obtain financial support for the Museum.

Because of the general scarcity of material on non-Jewish victims, the planning team included in the exhibition virtually all relevant exhibits it found in order to emphasize the principle of inclusion. And while the search for material continues, the fate of the non-Jewish victims in the Holocaust has now, after the opening, become one of the most important themes dealt with in the lectures and film programs organized by the Museum's Education Department, in the acquisition activities of library and archives, and in the work of the United States Holocaust Research Institute, the Museum's scholarly division.

In spite of a high degree of anti-German sentiment, especially among the survivor members of the Museum's lay leadership, German victims of Nazi persecution also found their place in the exhibition. As a matter of principle, the Museum did not accept money from the German government or from German corporations, but it did not exclude German victims from the Permanent Exhibition. German victims were included in the segments devoted to the persecution of the handicapped, homosexuals (only German homosexuals were persecuted by the Nazis), Jehovah's Witnesses, and Freemasons. The exhibition also contains German political anti-Nazi brochures and stickers from the prewar period. Beyond this, an entire segment is devoted to the "White Rose," the heroic group of idealistic students in Munich, Germany, who opposed the Nazi regime on moral grounds. The second of their seven anti-Nazi leaflets protested against the mass murder of Jews in Poland. They were caught, arrested, and executed. In addition, as already mentioned, the famous quote attributed to the German Protestant pastor Martin

Niemoeller summarizes, towards the end of the walk-through, the implied indictment of the bystander, which constitutes one of the main moral lessons to be learned from the exhibition.

The planning team decided, on the other hand, not to include in the exhibition the story of the conservative, elitist opposition groups in and around the army, who were involved in the unsuccessful assassination attempt on Hitler in July 1944. After that attempt most of their members were arrested and executed. They are today celebrated in Germany as martyrs of German anti-Nazi resistance. However, the moral fabric of their ideology and motivations, in which their fear that Hitler's inept military leadership might lead to Germany's defeat played an important role, did not warrant their inclusion in the section of the exhibition devoted to anti-Nazi resistance.

The inclusion of non-Jewish Holocaust victims was not in line with a thesis defended by influential Israeli Holocaust scholars, namely that the term Holocaust should be used only to refer to the annihilation of the Jews. This thesis was implicitly adopted by the survivors among the Museum's lay leadership. Their memory, experience, and mentality led them to advocate Jewish exclusivity. They wanted a "Jewish museum"—a museum that would tell the Holocaust story as a chapter of Jewish history only. It was difficult for them to share their painful memory with non-Jewish victims. However, all survivor members of the Museum Council participating in the creation of the Museum and its permanent exhibition accepted the principle of inclusiveness.

Pastor Martin Niemoeller, one of the leaders of anti-Nazi clergy in Germany.

FIRST THEY CAME FOR THE SOCIALISTS,
AND I DID NOT SPEAK OUT —
    BECAUSE I WAS NOT A SOCIALIST.

THEN THEY CAME FOR THE TRADE UNIONISTS,
AND I DID NOT SPEAK OUT —
    BECAUSE I WAS NOT A TRADE UNIONIST.

THEN THEY CAME FOR THE JEWS,
AND I DID NOT SPEAK OUT —
    BECAUSE I WAS NOT A JEW.

THEN THEY CAME FOR ME —
    AND THERE WAS NO ONE LEFT TO SPEAK FOR ME.

    attributed to Martin Niemoller (1892–1984)
    Anti-Nazi German Pastor

The report of the President's Commission on the Holocaust defined the Holocaust as "the systematic, bureaucratic extermination of six million Jews by the Nazis and their collaborators as a central act of state during the Second World War." The report recommended, however, that the Museum also include other exterminated groups, and that it deal with such issues as the collapse of the Weimar Republic, the rise of Nazism, and "the existence and culture of the Jews of Europe before and during the war . . . in order to recreate a vision of the world that was lost." Another theme that was recommended for inclusion in the Museum was "the reception of survivors after 1945 . . . and the response of renewed life after the events."

The recommendations delineated the thematic scope of the Museum and served as the planning team's guideline for composing the exhibition's story line and structure. Much of the strength of the exhibition lies in its thematic clarity, which led to a streamlined structure.

Obviously every definition implies negation. The thematic definition, focusing on the Holocaust, did not permit inclusion in the exhibition of other genocidal events. Though requests to incorporate other atrocities in the exhibition were met with sympathy, the planning team refused to deviate from the thematic definition outlined by the President's Commission and thus prevented dilution of the exhibition structure, content, and message.

Early on the planning team had to wrestle with the question of whether the Armenian massacres of 1915 should be presented in the Museum. Before the beginning of actual work on the exhibition, the United States Holocaust Memorial Council had adopted a resolution agreeing to such inclusion. The resolution, which resulted from pragmatic considerations, actually contradicted the thematic definition outlined in the President's Commission report. Once the resolution became publicly known, the Museum found itself under pressure from the Turkish lobby, which tried hard to prevent any mention of the Armenians in the exhibition. According to the official Turkish version, the anti-Armenian genocidal event never happened. The Israeli embassy lobbied on Turkey's behalf in this matter.

Opinions in the Content Committee were divided. The discussion was heated but did not result in a vote. Eventually it was accepted that, considering the thematic definition of the exhibition, it should not include a chapter on the Armenians. But in view of the promise that was given to the Armenian community, the Armenian massacres would be mentioned in the exhibition three times, strictly in the context of the Holocaust story: the first time the Armenians were to be mentioned in a quote from a speech by Hitler on the eve of the invasion into Poland, in which he said "who, after all, speaks today of the annihilation of the Armenians . . ."; the second time in a text panel which tells that Jewish resistance fighters in Poland were inspired by Franz Werfel's book *The Forty Days of Mussa Dagh*, a novel about Armenian resistance against the Turks; and on the "Rescuers Wall," in a biographical note about the photographer Armin Wegner who, during the First World War, took pictures of Turkish anti-Armenian atrocities. It was the thematic definition that motivated the vast majority of the Content Committee to reject the inclusion of an Armenian chapter in the exhibition.

A case in which the thematic definition shielded the integrity of the exhibition was during the German effort to persuade the Museum that it include a chapter on postwar Western Germany. The German Embassy in Washington feared that the exhibition might arouse anti-German feelings, and believed that a chapter on German restitution payments to survivors and on the financial aid it afforded the young State of Israel would at least partly counteract the negative impact of the Holocaust story. From the Museum's point of view, the addition of such a chapter would have been a mistake for two reasons. First, it would have been perceived as an attempt to downscale German guilt, as an inadvertent expression of forgiveness of behalf of the Museum. Second, it would have unreasonably extended the part of the exhibition devoted to the "aftermath." Moreover, not all of its postwar history, if honestly told, would shed favorable light on Western Germany—for example, its condoning attitude towards Nazi war criminals. The German embassy was told that postwar history fell outside the thematic definition of the exhibition.

The planners considered, however, whether they should include in the exhibition, at the end of the segment dealing with the war crime trials, a picture of Willy Brandt's *Kniefall* (German for genuflexion) in front of the Warsaw ghetto fighters monument, which was tantamount to an official admission of German guilt. The proposal came before the Content Committee and was vehemently opposed by all survivor members, who asked in whose name he made that gesture. They feared that including the picture might be perceived as granting forgiveness. And they did not feel entitled to forgive. The Director of the Museum retracted the proposal.

From the outset, the Museum played a role not only in the world of museums but also in a wider political sphere. The planners came to understand that by telling this particular story from the past they were dealing with the present.

At times, some staff members may also have thought that the exhibition should include other genocidal events: the middle passage of African slaves, the mass slaughters in Cambodia, or the plights of the Haitian boat people. It may have seemed that, to fulfill its mission, the Museum should deal not just with the past but also with contemporary issues that related to the themes of racism and genocide. It was inevitable that people who chose to deal with a subject matter as severe and sensitive as the Holocaust should view their work through the prism of their emotions and their moral, ethical, and political beliefs. Their strong compassion for the victims of the Holocaust was surpassed only by an even stronger compassion for the victims of their own time and with anger at the contemporary aggressors. Basically, this transposition of compassion and anger from the museum experience to the experiences of one's real life was, in fact, what the visitor was intended to undergo. However, to include other genocidal events (as did the Los Angeles Museum of Tolerance) would have been incompatible with the thematic definition of the United States Holocaust Memorial Museum.

An emotionally loaded debate among senior staff about the mission of the Museum questioned whether its mission lay in providing knowledge about the Holocaust as an event in history or in treating the Holocaust as a metaphor that could serve as a weapon in the struggle for human rights. The debate was labeled "the Museum as history or metaphor." In the heat of the discussion, some proponents of the metaphor-oriented position were not able to see that only a clear, accurate, and strong presentation of the Holocaust story as a chapter of human history would make it possible for individual visitors to understand by coming to it on their own how one should relate to "other holocausts." The Director took the position that any inclusion of additional thematic elements in the exhibition itself would weaken its focus and its potential to serve as a source of the metaphor, and thus as an agent of education about contemporary issues.

It is fair to assume that the passionate fervor of those staff members who wanted to incorporate contemporary events not directly related to the Holocaust in the exhibition was in some measure the outcome of feelings of helplessness and anger inevitably evoked in people who are so intensely occupied with the horrors of the Holocaust and are unable to do anything about it in real time, except by creating a museum.

Although inclusion of non-Holocaust elements would have blurred the Museum's focus, once the exhibition opened to the public, however, the Museum immediately began to develop activities that applied the lessons of the Holocaust to related contemporary issues of genocide and racism. These issues today play an

General Dwight D. Eisenhower at Ohrdruf concentration camp.

important role in the Museum's educational work among students and adults, as well as in its program of special exhibitions. The Museum's Public Programs Department, which deals with both education and exhibitions, has adopted programmatic guidelines that give high priority to programs dealing with contemporary issues, to "gray shadows of the Holocaust" haunting contemporary society. The guidelines also specify that in all these programs the link to the basic Holocaust theme should be always pointed out.

AMERICAN AND JEWISH ASPECTS

From the outset, there was a basic tension inherent in the project of creating the United States Holocaust Memorial Museum. Although a formal discussion never took place, there were clearly proponents of a "Jewish museum" and advocates of an "American museum" that would not be perceived as Jewish. Both apparently contradictory attitudes found supporters among lay leadership and senior staff.

The strongest proponents of the concept of a "Jewish museum" were among the survivors, who wanted the Museum to become primarily a memorial to the six million Jews who perished in the Holocaust that would project their pride in being Jewish. The survivors were joined in this by many leaders of Jewish institutions in the United States. Yet others wanted to prevent the Museum from being perceived as primarily a Jewish institution. Some believed that this would diminish the public

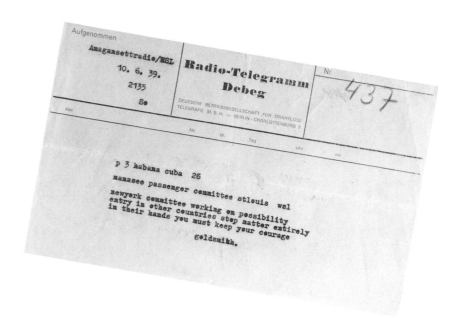

Top to bottom: Telegram sent by official of Joint Distribution Committee to refugees on the *St. Louis;* Jewish survivors at a displaced persons' camp look at posters in Hebrew, German, Yiddish, and English calling for Great Britain to open immigration to Palestine; U.S. Representative Sol Bloom with Assistant Secretary of State Breckenridge Long, discussing admission of refugees to the United States.

Israel's first Independence Day parade in Tel Aviv, May 14, 1948.

stature of the Museum and limit its attractiveness for non-Jewish visitors. They were afraid that a "Jewish museum" close to the National Mall might be regarded by the public as inappropriate or that it would arouse envy and resentment among other ethnic groups. Some influential senior staff members, Jewish and non-Jewish, further thought that the Museum's mission was of universal rather than of specifically Jewish character, and that this universal mission needed to be made explicit in the Museum's public image.

Such a polarization was inevitable because the Museum was, on one hand, a federal institution, mandated by an Act of Congress, and established in the heart of the nation's capital. On the other hand, the Museum's responsibility was to commemorate the Holocaust, the most terrible event in modern history, in which the majority of victims were European Jews. Reconciling this tension was one of the greatest concerns of the founding chairman, Elie Wiesel, during the years of his chairmanship.

Although the tension between the two different approaches was apparent from the beginning and found its expression in countless private conversations and utterances, it did not lead to an open controversy in the meetings of the United States Holocaust Memorial Council or its many committees—that is almost until the opening day. Shortly before the opening of the Museum, a fierce controversy about whether President Haim Herzog of Israel should be invited to speak at the opening ceremony split Council lay leadership into two camps: those who wanted him to speak, and those who thought this might cause the Museum to be perceived as a Jewish institution. The controversy was finally resolved by the White House: President Herzog was invited and spoke at the opening.

The planning team never discussed the problem of American or Jewish. Instead, it based its planning on the implicit assumption that the Museum has to be both American *and* Jewish.

The planners were aware that the Museum was intended to cater to Jewish and non-Jewish visitors from all over the United States and the world. To facilitate the emotional identification of American non-Jews with the Jewish victims of Holocaust, the story line was preceded by an introduction, at the very outset of the

Permanent Exhibition, showing American soldiers who at the end of the Second World War discovered and liberated concentration camps. This introduction defines the liberation of Holocaust concentration camps as an "American event." The American framework begins in the entrance hall with the display of battle flags of the American army divisions that took part in the liberation of camps and continues in the form of an audiovisual program in the elevator that carries the visitor from the Hall of Witness to the Permanent Exhibition floor. The exhibition opens with a picture of the visit of General Dwight D. Eisenhower to the Ohrdruf concentration camp accompanied by General Omar Bradley and General George Patton. This meeting of visitors with the American soldier was intended to immediately preempt any possible doubts about the relevance of the Holocaust to the American people.

In the course of the walk-through, visitors are confronted with the "American angle" many more times: in the exhibition segments dealing with the Evian Conference in 1938, at which the United States refused to help in solving the problem of the German Jewish refugees who had nowhere to go; the denial of entry visas to the refugees on the *St. Louis;* the refusal of the American army to bomb Auschwitz; the appointment of the War Refugee Board by President Roosevelt; the American soldiers liberating the camps in Western Germany and Austria; and the arrival of survivors in the United States after the war. There are also two large interactive facilities with ten programs, each six minutes long, illuminating various aspects of the response of the United States to the Hitler regime and the Holocaust, from the early 1930s and throughout the war. These programs are, in part, critical of the attitudes of the American government and the media. The government is accused of having for many years severely restricted access to the United States by refugees from the Nazi inferno and of having consistently refused to get involved in rescue activities until shortly before the end of the war. However, the critical programs are as relevant to America as are the laudatory ones. In fact, it is to the credit of American democracy that a federal museum located in the heart of the nation can raise such severe accusations against past American governments without evoking even one voice of protest.

The public success of the Museum, the ethnic composition of its visitor populations (which is composed largely of non-Jews), and the general tenor of reactions voiced by visitors clearly prove that the American public, with all its various ethnic groups, does indeed consider the Museum as relevant to the American nation.

On the other hand, the Permanent Exhibition clearly reflects the dominant Jewish aspect of the Holocaust. In addition to the strong Jewish presence embedded in the narrative, there are specifically Jewish segments, such as the monitor programs on Jewish life before the Holocaust, the tower room with photographic portraits by Roman Vishniak of Eastern European Jews, the struggle of the Jewish refugees to enter Palestine after the war, and the photo blowup showing the first Independence Day of the State of Israel.

The American and the Jewish aspect became so thoroughly interwoven in the story line of the Permanent Exhibition that it was accepted by both the advocates of an "American museum" and by those of a "Jewish museum." The two aspects were similarly balanced in the Wexner Learning Center and in the various educational programs of the Public Programs Department. The synthesis of the two aspects is, indeed, one of the basic characteristics of the Museum.

Yet the basic tension between the two approaches remains in the very character of the Museum. The tension will always be there because the contradiction is real and there is no way to make it disappear. Any attempt to force a showdown between the two attitudes will likely fail; more important, it would inevitably damage the Museum. A synthesis, a reconciliation, is possible in the actual Museum.

This tension surfaced in the heated argument about whether the Museum should be closed on Yom Kippur, out of respect for the millions of Jewish victims,

Arrival of Hungarian Jews at Auschwitz, 1944.

or whether it should remain open like all other museums on the Mall, so as not to be perceived by the public as a Jewish institution. The Museum did remain closed on Yom Kippur, and the decision did not hurt the reputation of the Museum as an American institution. On the other hand, a decision to leave the Museum open would have severely antagonized the organized Jewish community in the United States.

Since the opening of the Museum, there has been persistent pressure by survivors who demand that additional material on Jewish life and culture before the Holocaust be added to the Permanent Exhibition or, alternatively, that special exhibitions be made on such topics. However, the urge to enhance the Jewish element in the Museum cannot be satisfied without careful con-

sideration of existing balances. The Council's Chairman, Miles Lerman, who was appointed with the opening of the Museum, has steered a balanced course. While approving Museum participation in official American events such as the commemoration of the liberation of concentration camps and the dedication of the Eisenhower Plaza on the south side of the Museum, he has consistently opposed any measures that might diminish the Jewish substance of the Museum.

Even so, the survivors among the leadership of the Museum remain deeply worried about the future. They fear that once no survivors are around to fulfill the role of watchdogs, changes might be made in the Permanent Exhibition, the heart of the

Germans abusing Jews in Salonika, Greece, prior to their deportation to Auschwitz; Croat fascists torturing Serbian victim in Yugoslavia; Croat fascists ordering Jewish victim to remove his ring before being shot.

The ravine at Babi Yar, near Kiev, Ukraine, the site of mass executions of Jews.

Museum, that would upset the present balance of American and Jewish substance. And their fears may not be unfounded. The balance was consciously created by the architects of the institution who strove to build a museum that would be viable in spite of contradictory pressures. With changes in the relative strength of these pressures, future leaders of the institution may well be tempted to diminish the importance of the Jewish factor. However, there is a Latin saying—*habent sua fata libelli* (books have their own fates)—which means that once they come into the public domain, the author has lost control over them. The same is certainly true for museums.

COMMUNAL AND POLITICAL DEMANDS

Even after the opening, the inbuilt balances of the Museum are under constant pressures that are partly communal and partly of political character.

The omission of certain aspects of Holocaust history in the Permanent Exhibition provoked some of the communal pressures. Space limitation forced the planners to make choices: the major elements of the historical event had to be incorporated in the story line to the deplorable exclusion of others deemed to be more marginal. In certain cases, omissions can be redressed by inclusion of underrepresented aspects in public programs, and sometimes in special temporary exhibitions.

Some Hungarian Jews complained about the insufficient space devoted in the Permanent Exhibition to the tragedy of their community. Italian Jews similarly complained about the little space devoted to the rescue of Jews by the Italian army and population. Sephardic Jews complained about the alleged anti-Sephardic bias of the Permanent Exhibition. None of the complaints was entirely without justification. Basing the narrative on a sequential structure that refrained from elaborating on occurrences in specific countries occupied by the Germans prevented the planners from doing full justice to any of the specific communities, but while an exhibition based on a geographic structure might have been more satisfying to individual Jewish communities, it would have been a museological mistake.

Poland was the only country to which relatively much space was devoted—not only because it was by far the largest Jewish community in Nazi-occupied Europe (over three million Jews, ninety percent of whom were killed) but also because most European Jews who perished in the Holocaust were killed in the death camps that the Germans established in Poland. There was no way to weave an adequate narrative without focusing on Poland and on Auschwitz, the largest of the death camps, whose name has become a synonym for the Holocaust.

Another important criticism was that the Permanent Exhibition, in spite of the relatively large area devoted to Jewish resistance during the Holocaust, did not do justice to the great importance of this aspect in the overall picture. The Chairman of the Council, Miles Lerman, himself a former partisan who fought during the war in the forests of Southern Poland, was aware that no major changes could be made in the Permanent Exhibition; he therefore initiated the creation of a fund that would finance research about Jewish resistance in the Holocaust period.

More difficult to cope with were pressures that carried political overtones. To counteract the negative public image of Serbia, in view of the ongoing genocide in Bosnia-Herzegovina, Serbian circles demanded (in a mail campaign initiated by the Jewish-Serbian Friendship Association in the United States) the inclusion in the Permanent Exhibition of material about the Croatian genocide against the Serbians during the Second World War, to which they continually referred as "The Serbian Holocaust." At some point, the Museum was urged to display the government-sponsored exhibition on the Croatian death camp of Jasenovac in which the fascist Croat "Ustasha" murdered hundred of thousands of Serbs (in addition to more than twenty thousand Jews). The plight of the Serbians in the fascist Croat puppet republic during the Second World War was, indeed, hardly mentioned in the Permanent Exhibition. However, a special exhibition on the suffering of the Serbians in the Second World War, while genocide continued to be perpetrated by the Bosnian Serbs with direct or indirect support from the Serbian government, would necessarily have evoked undesirable political connotations.

On the other hand, the Museum was approached from different quarters with proposals for special exhibitions on current events in Bosnia. An exhibition of dramatic photographs, "Faces of Sorrow," was displayed in the Museum in the fall of 1994. The Museum considered it appropriate to raise its voice in this way against the genocide in Bosnia. The Prime Minister of Bosnia spoke at the opening. However, the Museum produced a brochure about the Holocaust in Yugoslavia, which told the story of Croatian and Bosnian collaboration with the Nazi regime and the mass murder of Serbians. The brochure linked the "Faces of Sorrow" thematically to the Holocaust. It was distributed to the visitors of the exhibition.

Yet another example of the manifold political pressures was in the demands presented by the high-level Ukrainian delegation, composed of leaders of the Jewish community and senior government officials, who visited the Museum several months after its opening. The delegation strongly voiced three requests. First, that a chapter on the "Ukrainian Holocaust," meaning the sufferings of the Ukraine and the Ukrainians during the Second World War, be added to the Permanent Exhibition. Second, that all references in the Permanent Exhibition to the Soviet Union be eliminated and replaced by references to the specific countries of Russia, the Ukraine, Belorus, and others as appropriate. Thirdly, that a chapter be added to the

Permanent Exhibition describing the sufferings of the Ukrainians under Stalin. It was the insistence of the planners on adherence to the basic thematic definition that protected the exhibition from being changed in response to political pressures.

Turkish pressures against the mentioning of the Armenian massacres of 1915 continued after the opening. The announcement of an evening devoted to the publication of a book with oral histories of Armenian survivors evoked objections from the Turkish embassy, which demanded the cancellation of the program. This demand was echoed in many letters the Museum received from Jewish personalities in Turkey. Naturally, in spite of the pressures, the program that aroused enormous interest among the Armenian community was not canceled.

More serious was the complaint by an evangelical Protestant minister who sent letters to all members of Congress alleging that the film on anti-Semitism presented on the upper floor of the Permanent Exhibition accused the Church of being responsible for the Holocaust. Although the minister was known in church circles as a fringe figure, the Museum received countless requests for explanations from Senators and Congressmen. The Museum's Church Relations Committee, composed of representatives from virtually all Christian denominations, upheld the legitimacy of the film. It recommended, however, that one sentence in the film's narration be modified, a sentence that could be misinterpreted as suggesting that one of the Gospels was distorting historical truth. The Museum accepted the recommendation.

THE MUSEUM AS A VOICE OF MORALITY

The Museum's political dimension has become inseparable from its professional success. Were it not for its unusual national and even international public resonance as a museum, nobody would attribute political significance to its public statements or the utterings of its leaders. However, the Museum is also a powerful statement of protest against racism, an outcry against genocide, and a warning against the dangers of fascism. It is widely expected to serve as a voice of morality in matters pertinent, or sometimes even only tangential, to its specific historical narrative. Thus in different ways the voice of the Museum was heard in public on such issues as the massacres in Rwanda, the "ethnic cleansing" in the former Yugoslavia, anti-Semitism in Poland, the discrimination against Gypsies in Germany, the killing of Kurds in Iraq, and other current world events.

The Museum's political potential is also an outcome of the unique power inherent in its character as a narrative museum. Collection-based Holocaust museums never have, and never could have, attained a similar level of public political significance. The fact that the Chairman of the Museum was among those invited by President Clinton to attend in Cairo the signing of the peace agreement between Israel and the Palestinian Liberation Organization, or that he was called to accompany the President on his visit to Poland, attests to his standing as a public figure.

When submitting its recommendations in 1979, the President's Commission on the Holocaust proposed that the United States Holocaust Memorial Council should, in addition to building a memorial museum, establish a "Committee on Conscience" composed of personalities of high moral standing. It would be the Committee's task to voice its concern whenever the specter of genocide raised its head. A Committee on Conscience was indeed created shortly after the appointment of the Council, but the Council then suspended it, probably because of a lack of clarity regarding the possible courses of action the Committee should adopt. After the opening of the Museum, the Council's Vice-Chair, Professor Ruth Mandel, was charged with heading an ad-hoc Committee to explore the feasibility of a Committee on Conscience. It eventually recommended that the Committee on Conscience be reestablished and function under the authority of the United States

Holocaust Memorial Council. Its mission was to alarm the public whenever actions of genocide or mass killings were perpetrated anywhere in the world, or when danger of such actions was perceived.

The creation of a committee whose declared task was to deal with events of political nature raised the questions of how a committee of a federal institution can express political opinions that might conflict with the policies of the government? Would the Committee have to ask for the State Department's permission whenever it intends "to raise its moral voice"? Was it free, for example, to demand the lifting of the arms embargo against Bosnia or to advocate American military intervention in that country, if the administration was known to oppose such steps? There was consensus that the Committee would refrain from advocating any concrete political steps and meticulously limit itself to the domain of moral statements. Its task would be to alert public opinion to the necessity of action. It could fulfill a meaningful role in the never-ending struggle against the perpetration of genocidal acts or mass killings, even if only by publicly raising its voice in protest.

The political function finds its most blatant, institutionalized expression in the Committee on Conscience. But in reality this function thoroughly permeates the life of the Museum and its perception in the eyes of the public, not only when public opinion is focused on genocidal events but also on an almost daily basis, and in multiple ways.

Inevitably, Council members have more personal interest in the public, political functions of the Museum than in its basic professional operation qua museum. Professional staff, on the other hand, are naturally closer to the museum function. In other museums, board members and other lay leaders have little, if any, involvement in the daily operation of the institution. They leave it to staff to run the museum. Not so in the Holocaust Museum. The Chairman and other leading Council members are deeply immersed in the political life of the institution and their involvement in various domains of the daily operation is intense. The cooperation between Chairman and Director borders on co-directorship, and the smooth functioning of the Museum depends on the ability of the Chairman and the Director to work together harmoniously.

It is of great importance that the balance between the professional and the political aspects of the Museum's work be maintained. It should never be forgotten that the political function is an appendix to the basic museological operation of the Museum, and not vice versa. "Overheating" the political aspect would, in the long run, damage its image as a professional museum and consequently impair its ability to function as a voice of morality in American society.

Along with its regular educational work, the Museum's moral-political activity is its most important mission in society: it not only depicts the historical narrative of the Holocaust, but it uses this museological depiction actively as a metaphoric warning, as a weapon in the battle against racist, ethnic, religious, and ideological hatred in all its human expressions.

THE ACTIVITIES: EDUCATION, COLLECTIONS, AND RESEARCH

IN PURSUIT OF THE EDUCATIONAL MISSION

The United States Holocaust Memorial Museum's purpose is to educate people of all ages, young and old, about the Holocaust. Its reason for being is its educational mission, which pervades all facets of the Museum's work, from the display of the Permanent Exhibition through the entire gamut of its activities inside and outside the Museum building. A visit to the Permanent Exhibition offers visitors their first exposure, overtly and subliminally, to the Museum's educational messages that are gradually transformed into emotions, assumptions, knowledge, and perhaps moral conclusions. The exhibition invites visitors to make distinctions that will relate these messages to their own personal experience.

The Permanent Exhibition is not the only tool used by the Museum for the purpose of education, however. To reinforce its educational impact, the Museum has developed a whole range of supplementary educational tools and activities: the Holocaust Library and the Wexner Learning Center for individual study, the Gonda Education Center with its classrooms for school classes and adult groups and its Educational Resource Center, the "Daniel's Story" exhibition for younger children, and a whole range of public programs for adult audiences, usually presented in the Joseph and Rebecca Meyerhoff Theater or in the Helena Rubinstein Auditorium. All these tools and activities serve to deepen the moral conclusions embedded in the Permanent Exhibition.

Surveys conducted periodically after the opening showed that between sixty and seventy-five percent of the visitors were non-Jewish. The great attractiveness for the non-Jewish population is obviously of greatest importance because it proves that the Museum has indeed succeeded in presenting the universal aspects of the Holocaust as a crisis of human civilization, and has avoided the danger of being perceived as relating to events of solely ethnic interest.

The surveys also illuminated that seventy to eighty percent of the visitors were college and university graduates and belonged to higher income groups. Between eighty and ninety percent were Caucasians; only a small fraction were African Americans, Hispanics, or Asians.

These figures reflect a deplorable aspect of the nation's cultural life in general, but for the United States Holocaust Memorial Museum they are alarming because of its mission to reach all social, ethnic, and religious groups with its educational message. Thus the Museum's Division of Public Programs (which organizes all the Museum's educational activities) keeps devising strategies of outreach into under-represented constituencies. A major step in that direction was made in 1994, when the Fannie Mae Foundation allocated a grant of one million dollars to finance a five-year educational program for the inner-city schools of Washington, D.C. A similar though somewhat smaller project was put into place for inner-city schools in Baltimore.

Long before its opening, the Museum was already regarded as a major center for Holocaust education in the United States. The Education Department received daily requests from teachers asking for help in teaching Holocaust history. After the opening of the Museum, the average number of requests came to more than one hundred per day. Some came by mail, phone, or fax, but many teachers visited the Museum personally to receive materials and information. Requests were received from around the nation. Some came from native people in Alaska, from the Amish in Pennsylvania, from reservation schools of American Indians, and some

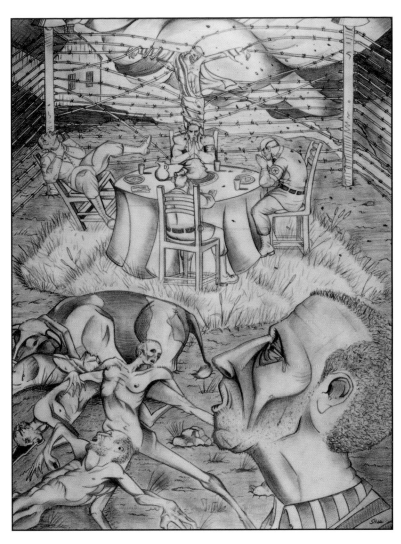

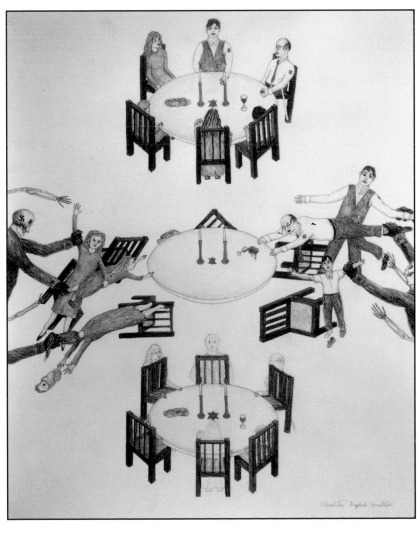

came from teachers and students at inner-city schools. The Museum's Educational Resource Center had to enlarge its staff to deal with the flood of requests.

The Museum has contributed to the professional training of Holocaust history teachers through periodical national and regional teachers' conferences that have been organized since long before the Museum's opening. In these conferences, academicians from within and outside the Museum lecture on Holocaust history and experienced Holocaust educators conduct workshops on methodological problems of Holocaust teaching. Sometime after the opening, a private foundation donated an endowment that will finance at least two such conferences annually.

Starting after Labor Day of 1993, school groups began arriving with their teachers to visit the Permanent Exhibition. In the first year, about 3,000 scheduled school groups and between 1,000 and 1,500 unannounced ones came to the Museum. Although the hope was for every scheduled group to receive an introductory orientation by one of the Education Department's teachers before the visit and, after the visit, to be invited to a "debriefing" session, in reality this happened with only about ten percent of the groups, mainly because of staffing shortages (but partly also because some of the groups did not have sufficient time left after the visit to the Permanent Exhibition, which normally takes about two-and-one-half hours).

One of the Museum's pre-opening educational outreach programs was the annual National Writing Contest, which invited junior and senior high school students to submit essays expressing their thoughts on the Holocaust. The first contest took place in 1984; for the 1994 contest more than five thousand students submitted written entries. The annual entries are judged by an independent jury composed of educators, historians, authors, and Holocaust survivors. Their judgment is based on originality, content, and quality of expression. First-place winners are invited to an awards ceremony, receive a set of books on the Holocaust, and are treated to a special tour of the Museum.

The entries are often amazing in their depth of understanding and strength of expression. The 1994 winner of the junior high school contest, Shoshana Wolf, an eighth-grader, submitted a poem that ends with the following lines:

> *I am the pen*
> *that will remain to teach the world*
> *to never forget this nightmare in history.*
> *For if this is forgotten*
> *this world will return to the land of nightmares.*
> *The land where children*
> *will die dreaming*
> *for a tomorrow*
> *that they will never see.*
> *Where mothers will cry out for a family*
> *that will never return.*
> *Where fathers*
> *will never live to mend*
> *their family in freedom,*
> *and where the dying*
> *will die forgotten*
> *I am a dreamer*
> *of the past, the present,*
> *and the future.*

In 1994, the Museum also began to organize an annual nationwide art contest for junior and senior high school students.

A unit of the Education Department was set up to arrange educational evening programs for adult audiences, which are usually well attended. The programs include courses in Holocaust history and Holocaust art; lectures and panel discussions on specific topics, usually with the participation of Holocaust scholars; and evenings devoted to newly published books or to contemporary humanitarian or political issues, with special attention to non-Jewish Holocaust victim groups. There are also film performances and musical evenings with programs of Holocaust-related chamber music. The Museum's educational activities for adults also include the numerous special events for organized audiences, which usually combine group visits to the Permanent Exhibition with lectures or discussions.

The adult evening programs constitute an important channel through which the Museum can deal with contemporary events. In 1994, for example, a series of programs was devoted to the events in Bosnia-Herzegovina, with the participation of the United States Ambassador to the United Nations, Madelaine Albright, and two former State Department officials who had resigned their positions because of disagreement with their department's policy regarding Bosnia. Another program dealt with the disaster in Rwanda.

Within a year after its opening, the Museum has become not only a central institution for schoolage Holocaust education, but also a vibrant cultural and educational center offering interested audiences a great variety of Holocaust-related programs.

REACHING OUT TO THE YOUNGEST

After consultations with numerous psychologists, the Museum decided to advise its visitors not to take children under age eleven into the Permanent Exhibition. The Museum offers, however, a special exhibition for younger children, eight years old and older, on its ground floor. The exhibition, entitled "Remember the Children: Daniel's Story" is, in fact, visited and enjoyed not only by young children, but also by many adults.

Consistent with the Permanent Exhibition, "Daniel's Story," which can be accessed directly from the Hall of Witness, is a narrative exhibition. The exhibition depicts the story of a fictitious young Jewish boy who lived in Germany during the Nazi period, was deported to the Lodz ghetto in Poland, and from there was sent to Auschwitz. In the camp he lost his mother and sister, but he and his father survived. Though fictitious, the story is based on real-life biographies and is accurate in all its historical elements. It can be assumed that the exhibition's great appeal to both children and adults is, at least in part, due to its narrative approach.

The creators of "Daniel's Story" found an appropriate way to tell the story of the Holocaust in a very explicit way to young children, making them understand what sad and difficult experiences Daniel had to go through. It is explicit without using graphic material that children of this age should be spared. The exhibition is based on three linked environments—Daniel's middle-class home in Germany, the room in which his family lived in the Lodz ghetto, and a room in Auschwitz—and two short video programs. Pages from Daniel's diary provide the explanatory text. Together with the Permanent Exhibition, "Daniel's Story" won a special award for design excellence at the 1994 annual convention of the American Association of Museums.

"Daniel's Story" was first displayed in the Capital Children's Museum in Washington, D.C., and a different version was presented as a traveling exhibition in Chicago. Several years before its opening, the United States Holocaust Memorial Museum redesigned it and took it to New York, Los Angeles, New Orleans, and

The exhibition, "Remember the Children:
Daniel's Story," presents Holocaust history
for children.

Young visitors in the Wexner Learning Center.

several other cities. Finally, a third version, based on the same narrative, was installed in the exhibition spaces next to the Hall of Witness for the opening of the Museum.

The idea of creating the "Daniel's Story" exhibition was originally conceived, and then fostered with much love, intelligence, and energy by Addie Yates, who chaired the Museum's Remember the Children Committee. Years before its opening, Addie Yates had organized the Museum's nationwide project encouraging young school children, who had been taught about the Holocaust, to express their reaction visually on ceramic tiles, with brush and paint. Three thousand such tiles were chosen to be installed as a colorful permanent Wall of Remembrance on the Concourse level of the Museum, opposite the classrooms of the Gonda Education Center. The Wall of Remembrance stands as a memorial to the million-and-a-half children who were murdered in the Holocaust.

Another of Addie Yates's Holocaust projects was the creation of a children's opening event that took place in the Joseph and Rebecca Meyerhoff Theater on the day the Museum was dedicated—a program of readings performed by nine talented young school children with much stage presence, who told about experiences of children in the Holocaust. The program also included the performance of a choir from the Adas Israel Synagogue in Washington, D.C. Just like "Daniel's Story," the children's opening event benefited adults as much as it did youngsters, and a year after the opening it was performed a second time.

LEARNING ON YOUR OWN: THE WEXNER LEARNING CENTER

One of the Museum's important educational instruments is the Wexner Learning Center, located on the second floor of the Museum building. While the visit to the Permanent Exhibition is a group experience, the visit to the Learning Center is an individualized one. In the Permanent Exhibition the visitor is surrounded by many people, mostly strangers, who move with him at a pace dictated by the flow of the crowd and the arrangement of the exhibits; he is constantly aware of the reactions to the displays by those surrounding him. The visit to the Learning Center, on the other hand, is an experience of withdrawal. Cut off from the environment by earphones, visitors undergo private learning experiences that take place between themselves and the screen in front of them. In contrast to the Permanent Exhibition, which imposes on visitors a narrative and confronts them with visual information chosen and composed by the Museum planners, the Wexner Learning Center offers a selection of information chosen by them, according to their own personal interest and absorbed at their own pace. Thus the Center constitutes an important complement to the Permanent Exhibition in its presentation of historical knowledge about the Holocaust.

The center is a sophisticated interactive computerized learning facility consisting of twenty-four networked computers that offer the visitor hundreds of illustrated articles from two encyclopedias: the *Encyclopedia of the Holocaust* in its entirety and selected articles from the *Encyclopedia of the Third Reich,* both published by Macmillan. By touching the sensitive screen, visitors can indicate the subjects about which they wish to receive information. Cross-referenced articles can be accessed by touching the highlighted term on the screen. Visitors can thus branch out from one article to another and come back to the previous one at will.

Articles in the Wexner Learning Center computers are enriched by illustrations drawn from five different data bases: still photographs, documentary film footage, video interviews with eyewitnesses, geographical maps, and music. Although the Center began operating the day the Museum was opened, its data bases continue to be enlarged with the help of photo and film experts, cartographers, and a musicologist whose expertise is Holocaust-related music. A year after the opening, the data bases held approximately 4,500 still photographs, 22 hours of motion pictures (documentary footage and oral histories), more than 500 maps, and about 10 hours of music—songs from the ghettos, the concentration camps, and partisans' groups.

The Center also affords the visitor access to a Holocaust chronology that offers information on a day-by-day basis about relevant historic events that took place during the Holocaust years.

The Center's technical system was designed and installed by an Israeli computer wizard, Yechiam Halevy, who joined the Museum staff for several years. Linking the twenty-four computers to one central computer, it is at the cutting edge of present-day technology for networked presentations and the retrieval of visual information. Even a year after the opening of the Center, no other comparable installation existed anywhere, and no company in the country had the know-how needed to design a similar one.

In the pursuit of the Museum's educational mission, the Wexner Learning Center hopes to reach out to the nation's school system. Though one cannot move the Permanent Exhibition, it would be possible to build outposts of the Learning Center in any school or college in the country, and it may even be possible to create branches of the Learning Center with direct access to the computer in Washington, D.C. The Museum is exploring such outreach possibilities, contingent not only on appropriate funding but also on the solution of rather complex copyright problems. Without doubt, the Wexner Learning Center eventually will build a wide network of identical study facilities outside the confines of the Museum building, thus becoming a pioneering installation in the use of the information superhighways.

Today the Wexner Learning Center is based on two programs: the illustrated Holocaust encyclopedias and the Holocaust chronology. However, there are broad possibilities for further program development. A collection of short documentary films could be made accessible through the Learning Center system. So could a collection of selected eyewitness video interviews with survivors, liberators, and perpetrators. A whole Holocaust atlas could be added. So could many other programs. The future development of the Learning Center is an open-ended project.

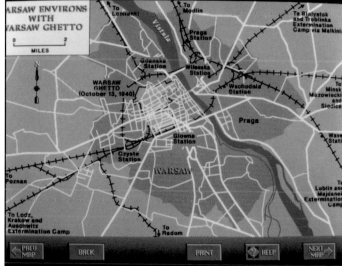

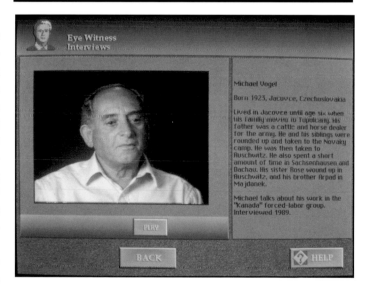

Computer monitor images from the Wexner Learning Center system.

The special exhibition, "Assignment Rescue: The Story of Varian Fry and the Emergency Rescue Committee," occupied the museum's lower-level gallery from the opening through April 1996.

Special, changing exhibitions are one of the yardsticks by which the success or failure of a museum's operation is measured. They reflect the museum's vitality and constitute the most important device to attract return visits. In a narrative history museum they are also the only way to supplement and amplify a relatively static Permanent Exhibition with additional historical information. The United States Holocaust Memorial Museum uses special, changing exhibitions to illuminate aspects of the Holocaust that were insufficiently covered, or not covered at all, in the Permanent Exhibition.

The only space the Museum has for the staging of major changing exhibitions is a 5,000-square-foot gallery on the Concourse level.

"Assignment Rescue: The Story of Varian Fry and the Emergency Rescue Committee," which opened several months after the opening of the Museum, told the story of a young American journalist who in 1940 was sent to Vichy, France, with a list of German and French writers, artists, and political activists who were in danger of being handed over to the Nazis. Varian Fry is one of the lesser-known heroes of this sad period. With considerable risk to himself, and in spite of the difficulties caused not only by the fascist Vichy authorities but also by the American embassy, which was opposed to his rescue activities, he succeeded over thirteen months in whisking more than 2,000 people out of France. These rescued people included many who were not on his original list but who came to his office in Marseille to ask for help. Among those he saved, before he had to escape from France himself, were the painters Marc Chagall and Max Ernst, the sculptor Jacques Lipshitz; the writers Leon Feuchtwanger, Heinrich Mann, and Franz Werfel; the surrealist poet Andre Breton; and many other outstanding representatives of Western culture.

A special exhibition on rescuer Oskar Schindler was displayed for six months in late 1994.

Varian Fry's heroic, successful rescue action was, until the exhibition opened, little known. The Museum awarded him the Eisenhower Liberation Medal posthumously. His children received the medal in a solemn ceremony that took place in 1991. In 1994, during the display of the exhibition, Yad Vashem, the Holocaust Martyrs' and Heroes' Memorial in Jerusalem, recognized Varian Fry as a "Righteous among the Nations," who risked his life to save the lives of others in the Holocaust. He is the only American among close to ten thousand rescuers who was honored in this way by Yad Vashem.

Like the Permanent Exhibition and "Daniel's Story," "Assignment Rescue" was conceived and designed as a continuous narrative. The many valuable objects and works of art displayed in the exhibition were integrated into the narrative. While planned and designed by a separate team, the Varian Fry exhibition remained faithful to the narrative style of the Permanent Exhibition. For 1995, the Exhibition Department planned two more major narrative exhibitions, one on Liberation to mark the fiftieth anniversary of the liberation of the concentration camps in Germany and Western Europe; the other on ghetto Kovno, to tell the story of a ghetto whose Jewish authorities fostered the spirit of anti-Nazi defiance.

Lack of sufficient adequate exhibition galleries has forced the Museum to be inventive in finding space for its smaller exhibitions, which were sometimes improvised on very short notice. After co-sponsoring the premiere of the film *Schindler's List* in Washington, the Museum covered a small wall, adjacent to the Wall of

Remembrance, with a mini-exhibition on Schindler, including authentic period photographs, a carbon copy of the original list, and the original violin played by Henry Rosner, one of the *Schindlerjuden,* at the parties Schindler gave for his Nazi cronies. Rosner survived and is now living in the United States. His violin was acquired for the Museum by three survivors who are themselves *Schindlerjuden.*

Further exhibition spaces had to be improvised for a photographic display mounted to mark the first anniversary of the Museum, as well as for the "Faces of Sorrow" exhibition about the genocide in Bosnia, which was mounted on temporary partitions between the Wall of Remembrance with its thousands of colorful tiles and the classrooms of the Gonda Education Center.

Special exhibitions are needed not only to supplement the basic narrative of the Permanent Exhibition or to apply its lesson to contemporary events. Through them the Museum can, for instance, present works of Holocaust-related art chosen by art experts. They can also be used to display objects from the Museum's collections that could not be included in the Permanent Exhibition.

THE SILENT WITNESSES

Before it adopted the narrative approach, the Holocaust Museum was conceived by its staff as a collecting museum. Staff aspired to build a museum that, while unique in content, would take its place as an equal among the other great national museums on the Mall, equal in character, equally dignified, and equally respected in the museum world.

Chamber concert of Holocaust-related music in the Joseph and Rebecca Meyerhoff Theatre.

As it collected artifacts, documents, and photographs, survivors and their children gradually began to regard the Museum as the repository, and perhaps the future showcase, for memorabilia from the days of the Holocaust. They brought passports, forged identify papers, ration cards, ghetto money from Lodz and Terezin, letters and postcards, snapshots from before and during the war—hundreds of objects which had witnessed and survived the Holocaust.

It was the silent assumption of the few museum professionals among the staff that eventually the collection of Holocaust-related objects would reach a size that would enable the Museum to use it as the material for a meaningful, collection-based permanent exhibition.

Once the narrative approach was adopted, and the worldwide search for relevant objects had begun, the collection began growing at a very fast pace. Thousands of artifacts were brought from Eastern Europe and Germany; at the same time, survivors and liberators—i.e., American soldiers who came to the concentration camps during the days of liberations—continued to bring to the Museum more and more of their memorabilia.

As a result, the Museum accumulated a collection of about 26,000 authentic Holocaust-related artifacts. (The actual figure is far larger, because in the Museum records similar victims' belongings—e.g., the four thousand shoes that are displayed in the Permanent Exhibition—are registered and counted as one item.) Less than one thousand items (again counting the four thousand shoes, etc., as one item) have actually been included in the Permanent Exhibition. Part of the collection is the property of the Museum, but a great part has been obtained by long-term loan agreements, most of which will probably never be terminated. It is today the largest collection of diversified objects related to the Holocaust.

Until the opening of the Museum, the Collections Department's main concern was to assist in the creation of the Permanent Exhibition by storing, recording, and preserving the incoming artifacts. The Department played a crucial role in the conservation of the objects as well as in their final installation. However, with the completion of the Permanent Exhibition, the role of the collection and the Collections Department in the framework of the Museum had to be reconsidered. A basic question arose: having opted for the narrative approach, was it necessary for the Museum to keep and develop a collection of artifacts? And if so, for what purpose? After all, the two historical museums in Israel, the Diaspora Museum in Tel Aviv and the Museum of the History of the City of Jerusalem, whose considerable public success had served as proof of the effectiveness of the narrative method, did not own any collections of artifacts.

In fact, generally speaking, a narrative history museum can fulfill its educational functions without a collection. However, in the particular case of the Holocaust Museum, a collection of objects was believed to fulfill a role of great importance, irrespective of the narrative Permanent Exhibition.

The Museum's 26,000 authentic Holocaust-related artifacts constitute a powerful argument against Holocaust denial and are important potential raw material for future research of Holocaust history.

Artifacts donated to the Museum by survivors: German identify card stamped with letter 'J'.

At the same time, the collection provides the answer to a strong psychological need of many survivors. Most Holocaust survivors are eager to preserve the various objects they saved, sometimes under great personal risk. They want to see these objects in public custody rather than disintegrating and getting lost in the attics of the homes of uninterested future generations. Often, after they have passed away, their children consider donating these memorabilia to a prestigious public repository as a way of showing respect for their parents.

Fostering close, understanding relationships with the donors of objects has, indeed, become one of the important, meaningful functions the Museum is fulfilling vis-a-vis the survivor community. The hundreds of survivor donors do not see their connection with the collection as concluded after they have delivered their objects and signed their deeds of gift. They relate to the Museum as a safe deposit box to which they have entrusted their valuables. Many among them continue to call the Collections Department in connection with their donations, to ask questions, perhaps to inquire about possibilities of display. It did not take long for the Department's staff to understand that in order to carry out their task they had to deal not only with artifacts but also, and even more so, with very sensitive human emotions.

Wooden toy made by inmate of Theresienstadt.

The Museum also acquires Holocaust-related art. Though no art has been included in the Permanent Exhibition, the enormous historical and cultural value of Holocaust art is recognized. By displaying it in the framework of special exhibitions, the Museum would add an important dimension to its educational work. In the years preceding the opening of the Museum, the Collection and Acquisitions Committee, in general, accepted only works of art that were created during the Holocaust period and therefore should be considered as historical artifacts. It postponed dealing with post-period art until after the opening, but it developed a registry of all post-period works that were presented to the

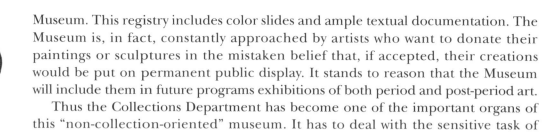

Museum. This registry includes color slides and ample textual documentation. The Museum is, in fact, constantly approached by artists who want to donate their paintings or sculptures in the mistaken belief that, if accepted, their creations would be put on permanent public display. It stands to reason that the Museum will include them in future programs exhibitions of both period and post-period art.

Thus the Collections Department has become one of the important organs of this "non-collection-oriented" museum. It has to deal with the sensitive task of donor relations, as well as with the storage, registration, cataloguing, maintenance, and conservation of the huge collection. In addition, it is fulfilling the vital function of exhibition maintenance in both the permanent and the changing exhibitions. This entails supervision of climate and humidity control in the exhibition spaces, periodical rotation of light-sensitive exhibits, and, naturally, continuous cleaning of all exhibits and surfaces. The Department is also responsible for all loan agreements with other museums and exhibitions, and for the transportation of exhibits to and from the Museum.

With the opening of the Museum, the staff of the Collections Department asked themselves whether their department would continue to play any role in the operation of a narrative museum, and if so, what that role would be. The question was legitimate. It has found its answer.

THE FIFTH FLOOR:
THE HOLOCAUST RESEARCH INSTITUTE

The fifth floor of the building houses the Holocaust Research Institute, the scholarly arm of the United States Holocaust Memorial Museum, which operates under the guidance of the Museum's Academic Committee. The Institute was opened in December 1993 with an international scholarly conference entitled "The Holocaust: The Known, the Unknown, the Disputed, and the Reexamined." The conference was attended by over one hundred Holocaust scholars from three continents. It catapulted the new institute into an important position in the international Holocaust research community.

A history museum can function perfectly well without an affiliated scholarly research institute. Conversely, a historical research institute can function perfectly well without being associated with a museum. But once they are linked to each other, they mutually determine their respective characters and modes of operation. The highly diversified structure of the Holocaust Research Institute and its archival collections stems from the unique character of the Holocaust Museum with its many-faceted educational and public activities that are served by the Institute's scholarly expertise.

Archival Collections

From the outset, it was a given that the Museum would include a research wing. Although its formal inauguration as a separate department occurred more than six months after the opening of the Museum, its foundations had been in preparation for many years. Everybody understood that, whatever the final character of the institute, the two basic instruments it would always need were an historical archives and a scholarly library.

The creation of the library was, in its first phase, mainly a matter of acquisition. The building of the archives, on the other hand, had to be carefully thought through because almost all authentic and historically important Holocaust-related

Doll belonging to Jewish child in the Krakow Ghetto.

archival material was in the possession of existing archives, and no archive voluntarily gives away original documents to other institutions.

Having gathered general information about the holdings of the most important Holocaust history archives on three continents, the Museum decided to build a system that would combine the catalogues of these archives in one all-encompassing computerized data base. This was clearly an undertaking of enormous dimensions, and in 1989 an alternative policy was adopted. The Museum decided to discontinue the work on the computerized international data base and to focus instead on the acquisition of copies of material from the governmental archives of the Soviet Union and the other Communist countries of Eastern Europe. These copies were to be obtained by an encompassing microfilming project.

During the preparations for the Permanent Exhibition, several other important archival collections came into existence: the Photo Archive, the Film and Video Archive, and the collection of interviews with Holocaust eyewitnesses. After the opening, all of them were organized as part of the Research Institute. Later, three more functional units were added: a Holocaust music collection, under the care of a musicologist; a unit responsible for the development of the Learning Center's data bases; and the Benjamin and Vladka Meed Registry of Jewish Holocaust Survivors. Academically, the most important element of the Research Institute is, perhaps, the direct support of research through fellowships, scholarly conferences, and seminars—a line of activity that the Institute began to pursue shortly after its opening conference.

The Institute's resident historians and various archival collections are constantly asked to provide professional advice as well as photographic, cinematographic, and musical material for various activities of the Museum, especially in education, public relations, exhibition, and publications. The Institute's departments are also in constant contact with scholars, writers, and publishers, with the media, and with various institutions and organizations who request information and visual material for a multitude of purposes. The textual archives, with its unusual material from Eastern European archives, is also beginning to serve the community of Holocaust scholars.

Each of the various component departments of the Institute is a world unto itself. The Holocaust Archives, which carries the name of the Ruth and Albert Abramson family, has copied, and continues to copy, documents mainly in Russia and Poland, but also in Belorus, Moldavia, Latvia, the Ukraine, Germany, the Czech Republic, and Romania. Most documents came from German sources. Though this extensive microfilming project in Europe became possible thanks to agreements signed many years before the opening of the Museum with the various Communist governments, it was and still is a very complex logistic undertaking. Each of the targeted archives is first visited by a group of competent scholars, mostly from outside the Museum staff, to determine which files should be copied. Then negotiations have to be conducted regarding permissions and payments; microfilming equipment has to be provided or obtained from local sources; staff has to be found; and finally the whole operation has to be constantly supervised. To run the operation, the Museum employs two regional project managers, one for all countries of the former Soviet Union, and one for Poland. Some of the work was carried out in cooperation with Yad Vashem, the central institution of Holocaust remembrance and research in Israel.

As a result of these efforts, more than two million pages of historic, Holocaust-related documents had been copied and brought to Washington two years after the opening of the Museum. These included important material that had never before been seen by Western scholars. Although after the disintegration of the Soviet Union many archives in Eastern Europe have become accessible to scholars, the concentration of two million pages of material, collected from so many different sources, in one central archive is of enormous importance for scholarly research.

The microfilming project operates under great urgency. In view of the political instability in most Eastern European countries, it is uncertain how much longer, and to what extent, archives will remain accessible. In some of the countries there are strong tendencies to prevent access to material that might incriminate people or organizations who during the occupation collaborated with the German invaders in the perpetration of war crimes. As of this writing in late 1994, much material can still be obtained, but no one knows how long this window of opportunity will remain open.

Concurrent with the acquisition of textual documents, the Museum has collected photographic and cinematographical material since the beginning of the preparations for the Permanent Exhibition. In the course of the preparations for the Permanent Exhibition, the Photo Archive accumulated over 40,000 images, which continue to be captioned and catalogued in a way that will make them easily accessible to the public and to staff. The Film and Video Department accumulated about 200 hours of documentary footage and hundreds of published Holocaust-related movies.

Since much Holocaust-related visual material is to be found in Eastern European archives, the acquisition activities of these two archival collections are conducted under window-of-opportunity pressures similar to those under which the textual archives operate. However, important visual material is also to be found in German, Austrian, French, Dutch, and other European archives, and the Museum has yet to begin developing an active acquisitions operation in these countries.

The Film and Video Department deals mainly with dissemination of information in reply to requests from within and without the Museum in addition to its job of acquiring film material. But it also has the professional expertise to produce fine educational audiovisual programs as demonstrated in the many prize-winning audiovisual components of the Permanent Exhibition, and the Education Department will eventually be able to make use of its production potential.

The Department of Oral History, which develops and maintains the collections of eyewitness testimonies, also works under great time pressure, though for different reasons. By now, more than half a century has passed since the Holocaust, and because of old age the number of witnesses—survivors, perpetrators, and liberators—who can be interviewed is swiftly diminishing. Since long before its opening, the Museum has been conducting hundreds of eyewitness interviews in the United States and has cooperated with Yale University in conducting interviews abroad, mainly in Israel, Poland, and the Ukraine, though on a smaller scale. Some interviews were also conducted among Jehovah's Witnesses and gay survivors in Germany and Holland.

Many Holocaust remembrance institutions and survivor groups in the country run audio and video interviewing operations of their own, but most of them deposit copies of their interviews in the oral history archive of the United States Holocaust Memorial Museum. As a result, the archive has become the second largest collection of Holocaust video testimonies in the world. A year after the opening of the Museum it counted close to 1,500 audio and close to 2,000 video interviews, out of which about 300 were produced by the Museum itself. The largest oral history video archive is held by Yale University, who were pioneers in the field.

The small musicological unit fulfills three major functions. It maintains a large and very valuable collection of Holocaust music, such as songs from the ghettos, the camps, and the forests, and also some orchestral music composed during the period, for example in the Terezin ghetto. It also deals, from time to time, with the production and publication of compact disks and cassettes with Holocaust songs. And it serves as advisor on all musical elements and aspects of the Museum's public and educational programs.

The Museum's aim is the integration of all departmental catalogues into one single super-catalogue that will enable the user to receive information on the holdings of all the various archival collections of the Museum. A researcher who wants to know what the Museum's archival collections have to offer on, for instance, Warsaw ghetto would find in this super-catalogue all textual documents, photographs, films, and eyewitness interviews on Warsaw ghetto that are in the possession of the Museum. Even the collection of artifacts and works of art, which are in the care of the Collections Department and in the Museum's various exhibitions, would be included.

Possibly the most precious department on the fifth floor is the Benjamin and Vladka Meed Registry of Jewish Holocaust Survivors. This Registry holds the names of close to 100,000 survivors and their offspring living in the United States, together with photographs and biographical information relating to the Holocaust period. Every other year, the names contained in the Registry are published by the Museum.

The Registry was created and developed almost single-handedly, over many years, by Benjamin Meed, a survivor of the Warsaw ghetto and the chairman of the "American Gathering," the organization of American Holocaust survivors. In 1993, the Registry was given to the Museum by the "American Gathering."

Most survivors, and relatives of survivors, who visit the Museum come to the fifth floor to search in the computerized Registry for relatives and friends. Many visitors ask for information on victims who perished in the Holocaust. Currently the Museum cannot provide such information. The largest encompassing, though not yet computerized, register of Holocaust victims is maintained by Yad Vashem, the Israeli Holocaust remembrance authority in Jerusalem. In coordination with Yad Vashem, the Museum's Registry of Jewish Holocaust survivors has now begun a major project of creating its own computerized register of victims.

Academic Programs

The Institute's mission is to foster research in Holocaust studies. The Museum's Academic Committee decided that the Institute should focus mainly, though not solely, on historiography and documentation of the Holocaust; ethics and the Holocaust; comparative genocide studies; and the impact of the Holocaust on contemporary society and culture. Additional fields of concern include refuge and rescue, and propaganda and mass media as they relate to genocide.

The basic approach is interdisciplinary. The Institute aims at drawing scholars in history, political science, philosophy, religion, sociology, literature, psychology, and other disciplines into its orbit. It maintains relations with academic institutions, museums, libraries, and archives around the world.

Since its opening, the Institute has focused its efforts on the creation of endowments that would enable it to award fellowships for scholars-in-residence and graduate students who would work in the Museum for varying periods of time. The first major scholar-in-residence program was endowed by a private foundation, the J. B. and Maurice Shapiro Charitable Trust. It provides funds to bring to the Museum senior scholars who stay for periods of up to one year to write and study. During their residence period they also give lectures at universities throughout the United States and act as a resource for the Museum and the public. The fellowships are awarded on the recommendation of the Museum's Academic Committee. Shortly after the announcement of the J. B. and Maurice Shapiro fellowship, endowments and funds for additional fellowship programs were obtained from other donors. The Institute also convenes scholarly conferences, seminars, and public lectures in the framework of its academic programs, sometimes in cooperation with the Education Department.

Publications

The Institute also runs a publishing program that intends to give priority to out-of-print classics, new works of special merit, survivors' accounts, collections of documents, etc. Emphasis is also placed on scholarly studies that, though essential to an understanding of the Holocaust, are not commercially viable. The first publications included a book by Dr. Michael Berenbaum, the Director of the Research Institute, entitled *The World Must Know: The History of the Holocaust as told in the United States Holocaust Memorial Museum.* Another book was *Resistance* by Professor Israel Gutman, an account of the Warsaw ghetto uprising in 1943; the third, *Anatomy of the Auschwitz Death Camp,* an anthology consisting of twenty-nine essays written by outstanding scholars from the United States, Israel, and Europe. All these books were published by arrangement with commercial publishing houses. An important forthcoming publication presently in preparation is a Holocaust Atlas, based on the maps of the Wexner Learning Center.

The Museum also publishes, in association with Oxford University Press, a scholarly periodical: the "Journal of Holocaust and Genocide Studies." The editorial board is composed of eminent Holocaust scholars from the United States, Israel, and Europe.

Not all publications of the Museum are of a scholarly nature and published through the publication unit of the Research Institute. The Departments of Education and Communication also generate publications. Thus, for instance, the Museum published a novel for children, *Daniel's Story* by Carol Matas, reprinted a book written by Varian Fry, *Assignment Rescue.* It also published a children's version of *The World Must Know,* under the title *Tell Them We Remember,* written by Susan Bachrach. Even before its opening, the Museum published a second version of a Holocaust classic, *I Never Saw Another Butterfly,* a collection of children's drawings and poems from the Terezin ghetto. A book under the same title was published in 1978 by Schocken Books, but the one published by the Museum includes many drawing and poems which were not included in the first version. It appeared with a foreword by Chaim Potok and an afterword by Vaclav Havel, president of the Czech Republic.

THE PEOPLE WHO DID IT

Many people participated in the creation of the Museum. They can, perhaps, be divided into three main groups: the staff, the lay leadership of the Council, and the numerous supporters throughout the country. Only the cooperation of the three groups could have made the dream come true. The supporters contributed encouragement, advice, belongings, and the necessary funds. Council members determined institutional policies; they conducted the successful fund-raising campaign; they guided the construction process of the building and made all related contractual and financial arrangements; they wove the network of intergovernmental agreements and developed the political dimension of the Museum; and they mobilized the crucial support of the survivor community.

However, the daily work in the creation of the Museum was carried out by hundreds of staff members. Who were these staff members, where did they come from, and what did they experience in the course of their work for the Museum?

They were a colorful group of people who came from different disciplines. Among them were historians, sociologists, educators, filmmakers, computer experts, architects, archivists, and people from numerous other professions and disciplines. It attests to the unique character of the Museum that few among them had any previous professional museum experience.

Staff members came from different countries, had different ethnic and religious backgrounds, and adhered to different beliefs and philosophies. However, all were soon united in extraordinary devotion to a joined mission that touched on the most basic facets of human existence. The feeling that they were fulfilling a mission rather than just working to make a living was shared by Jewish and non-Jewish staff members alike.

As it turned out, most staff members shared a high level of social consciousness and were very sensitive to phenomena of discrimination and injustice in society. Dealing daily with the visual raw material of Holocaust history, they found themselves under severe emotional pressure. It is astounding how they succeeded in retaining their sensitivity without becoming paralyzed by the subject matter, how they reached a certain level of immunity without losing their openness to the material with which they had to deal. Perhaps it was the feeling of belonging to a group engaged in the pursuit of an unusually important social mission that protected them and gave them the strength to cope with their creative work. However, the emotional pressures led to tensions—emotional tensions experienced by individuals and tensions within the group.

Within a short period of time staff had to undergo three major transitions. First was the transition from a fragmented organization to an integrated institutional structure. Then came the transition from a museum in the planning and building stage to an operating museum. Last was the transition from an institution financed mainly by private donations to an institution receiving substantial federal appropriations and obligated to abide by all bureaucratic rules of the federal administration.

Until about a year before its opening, the Museum was divided into three independent organizational units, each of which had its own director and reported to a different lay leader: the "Museum," the "Campaign," and the "Council" (a division that included a group of unrelated activities, such as finances, outreach education, and public relations). Additionally, there was a small, independent architectural unit that dealt with construction. The closer the Museum got to its opening, the clearer it became that without integration of the different divisions within one unified organizational structure it would be impossible to bring the process to its successful completion. The Museum needed a unified structure and a unified chain of command in order to achieve the necessary close coordination between the various departments and the indispensable horizontal staff cooperation across the lines of the various divisions.

It was the initiative of senior staff that started the process that eventually led to the present institutional structure. The restructuring succeeded, but it did not come about without difficulties and tensions.

It is well known that transitions are always difficult times in the life of an organization. The expectation of change involves uncertainty about what may lie ahead. Even when the transition is in line with anticipated development, the prospect of having to abandon the position in the organization one has become accustomed to in itself evokes anxiety and tension. With major transitional changes lying ahead—becoming an operating museum and adopting federal rules of procedure—senior management had to take into account the difficulties that staff would go through as an essential part of the changes they were to enact.

Even three months before the opening, many competent staff members did not believe that it would be possible to complete the preparations on time. Staff worked around the clock and made superhuman efforts to make the impossible possible. The high tension of these efforts that preceded the opening converged with anxieties that stemmed from two main sources: the anticipation of change in personal position, role, and task; and the anticipation of meeting the museum visitor.

According to the nature of their respective tasks, many staff members were expected to leave the Museum once the planning and building phase was over. However, most of them had the ardent with to continue a working relationship with the institution. It was not easy to leave the place where one had invested so much of one's soul. Management tried to integrate all those who wanted to continue working with the Museum into the new organizational structure. Thus many staff members had to switch to entirely different tasks, often demanding training for work they had never done before.

Essentially, everybody had to be trained anew, to be prepared for functioning in the framework of an operating museum, with masses of visitors daily invading the building, its exhibitions, and its many facilities. Unconsciously everybody expected the effort towards the opening event to be followed by a breathing pause for rest and training towards operation. But this was not what happened. In reality, from the first day on, trained or not, the staff was overwhelmed by the need to cope with thousands of visitors every day, to operate a complex building whose many high-tech systems had never been tested in real action, and to fulfill countless functions for which they were not totally prepared. Moreover, the Museum was severely understaffed, partly because of the attempt to stay within an unrealistic Council-mandated budget and partly because the number of visitors exceeded by far even the most optimistic expectation. What was perceived by the visitors and the media as a smoothly running operation of vast dimensions was for the staff one of the most difficult periods.

In this extremely difficult situation, it was the then Deputy Director of the Museum, Elaine Heumann Gurian, who played a most critical role. Having come to the Museum about a year and a half before the opening, Ms. Gurian applied her great organizational talents and rich museum experience to the preparation of the manifold administrative and technical systems underlying the operation of a large museum, and it was she who navigated the staff through the stormy initial phase. She brought to the Museum several experienced professionals, some as temporary consultants and some as regular department heads. One of the important organizational tools she created, with the help of a colleague transplanted from another museum, was the Department of Visitors Services, which cares for all aspects of the Museum's meeting with its visitors.

The gradual development of an operational routine and the process of training-while-operating was complicated by the third transition, namely the transition to all-pervading federal rules and bureaucratic procedures. It affected all levels of the operation and required specialized staff training that, in fact, continued long after the opening.

With the opening of the Museum a great project was brought to completion. Until then all work was project-oriented. Nothing was routine, everything was new, creative. Now had come the time to define, beyond the daily routine, new targets. To each department quarterly and annual goals and objectives were assigned. The ways and means were determined by which the Museum would fulfill its educational public mission. Here, again, a relatively new organizational tool was created that had proved in several other museums to be very useful: a Division of Public Programs, responsible for all educational programs, both for children and for adults, and for the supervision of Visitors Services, Exhibitions, and Collections. The Division of Public Programs became the heart of the operating museum. It was headed by Sara Bloomfield, who for many years had been the successful Executive Director of the United States Holocaust Memorial Council. Of her own will, she gave up her prestigious position in order to devote herself to the "heart of the matter." Public Programs together with the Research Institute, headed by Michael Berenbaum, are the two outreach arms that carry the Museum's message to the world.

Time and again members of the staff expressed their feeling that their work in the creation of the Museum was the most important thing they had done in their lives. This sentiment was shared by most members of the leading group of lay leaders.

THE THOUSANDS OF FEET *that make this pilgrimage of horrid re-membrances, and the millions of tears they cry, will never make amends for those who perished. Only if those thousands of feet keep walking to ensure that the sins of men will not be repeated will this place bring justice to us all.*

These words were written into the Book of Comments, at the end of the Permanent Exhibition, by one of the two million visitors who came to the Museum during its first year. The book is filled with similar comments. They corroborate the thesis that the United States Holocaust Memorial Museum is a museum of a different kind, a museum that makes its visitors understand the relevance of its Holocaust-related historical content to events and problems of contemporary life. Many visitors leave the Museum with this understanding, and some of them expressed it very strongly in the Book of Comments:

They cried "**NEVER AGAIN**"
But what about Bosnia
what about Rwanda
what about Haiti

But there is more than one lesson to be learned from the history of the Holocaust. Every visitor carries away his or her own lessons. Another visitor made the following entry into the Book of Comments:

SUCH THINGS HAPPEN *not only because of bad people, but because good people stand by and do nothing.*
And some more reflections from the Book of Comments:

I AM SORRY *I had to learn of the Jewish history this way. Nothing compares, no words can express what I feel in this moment, my only words are tears . . . tears . . . tears . . .*

Another visitor observed:

I SAW A PICTURE *of a four-year-old boy reading a book. Later he was killed. Might this little child have been the man who found a cure for cancer fifty years later had he survived?*

And yet another expressed, perhaps in the best way, what the Museum tried to achieve:

I AM SPEECHLESS. *The exhibits bring the Holocaust to a deeply personal level. There is much I will never understand, but this place is the beginning.*

Finally, a comment included in a personal letter written by the President of the United States, Bill Clinton, to the Director of the Museum, after a tour of the Permanent Exhibition:

. . . A FEW MOMENTS OF QUIET STUDY *outside the White House are a rare privilege. Your tour deeply touched me and changed forever my understanding of the tragedy of the Holocaust and of the singular acts of heroism that should affirm our hope for humanity.*

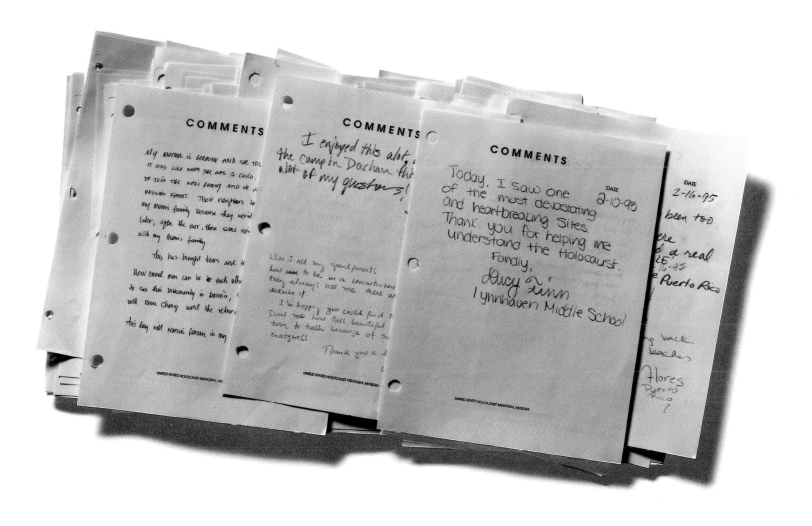

Pages from books of visitors' comments.

PHOTO CREDITS